Praise for *No Fear of Failure*

"*No Fear of Failure* whisks readers into the executive suites, board-rooms, battlefields, and football fields—all the places where great leadership is imperative. It's a must-read for any executive, in a climate when leadership has never been needed more."

—Ali Velshi, chief business correspondent and weekday host, CNN

"With brilliance and clarity drawn from firsthand experience with some of the world's most celebrated leaders, Gary Burnison has written one of the most important and useful books for 21st century leaders. It will soon be referred to as *The Global Guide to Successful Leadership*."

—Warren Bennis, Distinguished Professor of Business, University of Southern California; author, *Still Surprised: A Memoir of a Life in Leadership*

"*No Fear of Failure* offers riveting insight on leaders who lead by example, who recognize the importance of trust, and who under-stand that leadership is about earning the right to have others put their trust in you and then live up to that responsibility every day. It's a powerful book that provides insightful inspiration to any leader."

—Tim Flynn, global chairman, KPMG

"Gary Burnison has assembled an all-star cast to explore what it takes to be a leader today. As the profiled leaders attest, having 'no fear of failure' allows leaders to move forward knowing that they will not always win, with the understanding that the real victory is in the lessons learned from all experiences, positive and negative."

—Harry M. Jansen Kraemer, Jr., former chairman and CEO, Baxter International; author, *From Values to Action*

NO FEAR
of
FAILURE

NO FEAR
of
FAILURE

Real Stories of How Leaders Deal with
RISK AND CHANGE

～ GARY BURNISON ～

JOSSEY-BASS
A Wiley Imprint
www.josseybass.com

Published by Jossey-Bass

A Wiley Imprint

989 Market Street, San Francisco, CA 94103-1741—www.josseybass.com

Jossey-Bass books and products are available through most bookstores. To contact Jossey-Bass directly call our Customer Care Department within the U.S. at 800-956-7739, outside the U.S. at 317-572-3986, or fax 317-572-4002.

Jossey-Bass also publishes its books in a variety of electronic formats. Some content that appears in print may not be available in electronic books.

Library of Congress Cataloging-in-Publication Data
Burnison, Gary, 1961-
  No fear of failure : real stories of how leaders deal with risk and change / Gary Burnison.
    p. cm.
  Includes index.
  ISBN 978-1-118-00078-6 (hardback), 978-1-118-02304-4 (ebk),
978-1-118-02305-1 (ebk), 978-1-118-02306-8 (ebk)
  1. Leadership. 2. Risk management. 3. Organizational change. I. Title.
  HD57.7.B867 2011
  658.4'092—dc22

                                                                    2010051336

Printed in the United States of America

First Edition

HB Printing
10 9 8 7 6 5 4 3

To my wife, Leslie,
who has had by far the biggest influence on my life,
and who reminds me that it is not what you do,
but who you are, that matters most

CONTENTS

ACKNOWLEDGMENTS

Bringing together a book of interviews with outstanding leaders on three continents was hardly a solo effort. There are people I would like to acknowledge for their contribution to our firm and for their impact on my life.

First and foremost to my immediate family: my wife, Leslie, and my children, Allison, Emily, Jack, Olivia, and Stephanie, for continually showing me true north. Thank you, Leslie, for continually reminding me to separate what I do from who I am. As CEO I am ultimately responsible for leading and guiding this team, this organization. But I am a person first—husband, father, friend, colleague—and always.

To my extended family: my dedicated colleagues at Korn/Ferry for living every day our firm's mission of enhancing the lives of our clients, candidates, and colleagues. Success in any organization is only achieved through people; at Korn/Ferry, this is no exception. I will forever be indebted to the people of Korn/Ferry. Thank you for pushing our firm to the stars.

To the visionaries and founders of Korn/Ferry: Lester B. Korn and Richard M. Ferry, who created a firm that has changed thousands and thousands of lives. To the Korn/Ferry board of directors for their stewardship. To former chairman Paul C. Reilly for showing me what leadership means.

To those who helped secure the interviews for this book: Scott Coleman, Al Delattre, Robert Eichinger, Michael Franzino, Yue Guo, Jack Lim, Sam Marks, Horacio McCoy, Tierney Remick, Michael Rottblatt, Don Spetner, Eduardo Taylor, Stephen Trachtenberg, and Charles Tseng.

To those who worked very hard to make this book happen: Michael Distefano, for going all nine innings as part of the interview team; Dan Gugler, for always taking the midnight train; Tricia Crisafulli, for her passion for the journey (and for her dedication to getting the words on the page); Dana Martin Polk, for his commitment; and Joel Kurtzman, for insight as this book came together.

To our publisher, Jossey-Bass: our editor, Karen Murphy, for skillful and thorough editing; and the team of Erin Moy, Gayle Mak, and Mark Karmendy.

Last, my heartfelt thanks to the leaders who graciously shared their wisdom and experience: Michael Bloomberg, Eli Broad, Drew Gilpin Faust, Vicente Fox, Franklin "Buster" Hagenbeck, Olli-Pekka Kallasvuo, Liu Chuanzhi, John McKissick, Anne Mulcahy, Indra Nooyi, Carlos Slim, and Daniel Vasella.

For these leaders, it was not just what they said, it was how they made you feel.

If your actions inspire others to dream more, learn more, do more, and become more, you are a leader.
—John Quincy Adams,
sixth U.S. president

INTRODUCTION: LEADING THE WAY

Leaders have always faced an array of challenges, opportunities, and decision points. Gone, however, are the old ways of thinking that centered on growth driven by an insatiable Western consumer. New ways require a higher level of innovation, creativity, and strategic thinking. How, then, can leaders succeed in this new normal?

To answer this question, I embarked on a journey in 2010 to engage in discussions about leadership that took me and my team literally around the world: talking with leaders in the Americas, Europe, and Asia. Our search was for extraordinary leaders to share their thoughts and views about what it means to lead and what it takes to inspire others to follow. We spoke with leaders on three continents: several CEOs, a highly successful entrepreneur who is also the richest man in the world, a military general who led U.S. troops in Afghanistan, the mayor of New York, the former president of a sovereign nation, and America's most winning (by a mile) football coach. Virtually all are well known on the world stage with success stories that we've been privileged to witness over the years. Some we were meeting for the first time.

In every conversation, I was struck by an overarching commonality: each leader exhibited tremendous courage around the possibility, and even the inevitability at times, of failure. In the face of such uncertainty, they draw on an inner strength that allows them to strive for what is possible rather than become paralyzed by the risk of failure.

Having no fear of failure does not imply that leaders have never failed or that they will not fail in the future. It does not equate to brashness or bravado. If anything, it is the opposite. The famous basketball coach John Wooden once said, "Success is never final, failure is never fatal. It's courage that counts."[1]

No one knows that better, perhaps, than Lieutenant General Franklin L. "Buster" Hagenbeck, who in 2002 led his troops to battle foreign al-Qaida in brutally harsh winter conditions along the border of Afghanistan and Pakistan. "The right kind of leaders will accomplish the mission without taking unnecessary risks with their subordinates," he told me when we met at West Point.

Vicente Fox risked going up against the predominant political party in his country, the Institutional Revolutionary Party (PRI), even though there could have been reprisals against the family's ranch and other landholdings. Rather than retreat quietly, Fox campaigned for office and became the first opposition president, ending seventy-one years of the PRI regime in Mexico.

With a dream of building affordable homes, Eli Broad took the risk of offering consumers an innovative design. Despite the naysayers, Broad stayed true to his vision and later went on to found two Fortune 500 companies. Today, he is a billionaire philanthropist.

With courage to face seemingly insurmountable obstacles posed by China's centrally planned economy, Liu Chuanzhi dreamed of creating a company that he hoped would one day become the IBM of China. He started a company with only eleven employees. Twenty years and many obstacles later, Liu's company, Lenovo, bought the personal computing unit of none other than IBM.

As the extraordinary leaders in this book illustrate, having no fear of failure is a prerequisite for leadership. But where does such fearlessness come from, allowing leaders to charge ahead?

How do they inspire those who follow them to handle the risks and uncertainty and stretch beyond what they thought was possible?

It takes self-confidence and bravery to reconcile oneself to the fact that every big effort does come with the risk of failure or disappointing results. During our initial conversation, Olli-Pekka Kallasvuo, who was then CEO of Nokia, identified courage as the most important quality because leaders always face the possibility of failure. Several months later, OPK, as he is known, stepped down from his position at Nokia, exhibiting the grace of a true leader for whom the outcome was not what he had planned, yet he remained loyal and committed to the company where he had spent more than thirty years.

The potential of experiencing failure at times cannot keep leaders from pressing on with the pursuit to make and seize opportunities in a truly global marketplace. Hunkering down and hiding is never an option, not even in difficult times. At Korn/Ferry International, we faced that challenge during the global financial crisis. Although we felt deeply our clients' retrenchment and decline in spending, our response was to expand, not contract. We sought opportunities to preserve our brand and accelerate our future growth, including completing three strategic acquisitions. As a result, by early 2010, we were able to report strong growth in our business, significantly outpacing our industry.

As I reflect on my own experiences and those of other leaders, I am struck by the fact that even when highly successful, everyone has some degree of previous failure as a common denominator. For most of us failure is temporary; it passes like a storm. Why, then, should we let fear paralyze us? What are we really afraid of? Is it that our egos can't stand the possibility of failing? The real questions to contemplate are what greater accomplishment or goal could be achieved if we did not give in to our fears? What are others able to achieve that we are not because they do not view failure as terminal?

The most important aspect of failure is not the moment of defeat or loss. Rather, it is what happens the moment after failure occurs and a choice is presented: to allow fear to rule or to shift from setback to lesson learned. Henry Ford said, "Failure is the opportunity to begin again more intelligently."[2] I don't know a CEO who can't identify with that sentiment, knowing that it takes both success and failure to shape one's ability to lead. Success may instill confidence, but it is failure that imparts wisdom. With wisdom comes the inner serenity needed to create a bridge between failure and success.

Our work at Korn/Ferry in talent development, combined with our method for identifying high-potential and emerging leaders, has produced some fascinating discoveries of what distinguishes a great leader who truly makes a difference from a good leader who is competent. Great leaders are comfortable with ambiguity, paradox, social complexity, and change. They are not only willing but also interested in exposing themselves to first-time experiences, trying and sometimes failing and learning from their mistakes.

When leaders are fearless in the face of potential failure, their curiosity, openness, and courage make it possible for them to keep learning long after they've mastered their craft. Comfort with self is balanced by a high degree of social attunement, which often involves listening closely and responding appropriately to the needs and motivations of others, building effective teams, understanding others, and being accessible.

Although the leaders we spoke to had varying styles, strengths, and personalities, they were anchored in several characteristics. I call these qualities the "what" and the "how" of leadership. The "what" refers to what leaders must do to lead an organization—in other words, their roadmap or strategic framework. These leaders establish a unifying purpose around the vision and mission of the organization. They create a strategy to achieve the vision, identify and develop people to execute the strategy, measure and monitor the progress of the strategy, empower and inspire people, and reward and celebrate the accomplishments along the way.

The "how" of leadership means how leaders go about doing the things that they must engage in continuously. They anticipate, navigate, and communicate; they listen, learn, and then lead. You will see these verbs employed throughout our discussion: how leaders anticipate change; navigate through difficulties; communicate mission and purpose; listen more than they talk; commit to lifelong learning; and then, from the basis of all these things, lead their teams to victory. Through these common attributes, leaders implement and execute strategies with confidence and move forward with no fear of failure.

THE PEOPLE BUSINESS OF BEING A LEADER

Although leaders must be able to face risks and battle the odds, they cannot succeed without a talented team of followers. This is why leaders are in what I call the "people business." Highly effective leaders live by the fact that people are truly their organization's most precious resource. Attracting, developing, and retaining talent is paramount.

It has been said that 90 percent of strategy is execution, and 90 percent of execution is based on people. Despite all of the technological innovations of the past century a simple truth remains: people make businesses successful. People are the instruments of change. With the right people on his or her team, a leader has greater courage to take calculated risks.

New York City mayor Michael Bloomberg executes his strategy by empowering the talented individuals who want to work for him at city hall. "You couldn't [recruit] half of these people [to come] here or anywhere else if you didn't delegate," Bloomberg told us. Giving subordinates authority and responsibility builds the team and raises the level of each person's contribution.

Although the people side of a business seems straightforward, it is extraordinarily complex. It is not just a question of hiring talented individuals. More important is ensuring that the people are linked to a purpose that is greater than any one individual.

John McKissick has amassed more football victories than any other coach on the high school, college, or professional level. With such success, it's not surprising that, at times, he may have as many as one hundred players on his squad at Summerville High School in Summerville, South Carolina. McKissick's job as the leader is to turn each individual, whether the star player or the third stringer, into part of a disciplined, cohesive team.

A leader builds a team through competency and caring. With competency, leaders demonstrate the depth of what they know, which instills confidence in followers. At the same time, when followers know that the leader cares about them personally, they, too, become fearless and will take the necessary risks to accomplish a mission. In war, those risks are literally life and death. "When the soldiers know you care for them, and they know you are competent, they will literally put their lives on the line for you," Hagenbeck added.

Motivating and managing a team requires that leaders have a high degree of emotional intelligence. As a physician and an empathetic listener, Daniel Vasella learned to read the unspoken communication of body language and emotion that is part of any interaction. Later as CEO and now as chairman of Swiss pharmaceutical company Novartis, he used his awareness to understand how people's emotions—especially fear and anger—have the power to influence perceptions, decisions, and behaviors.

Vasella also demonstrated another important ability shared by leaders who are admired and accomplished: they know themselves. They understand that leadership begins with who they are as people—their honesty, humility, and integrity—and it ends with personal accountability for failure and team recognition of success. In between are long hours, passion, a relentless and insatiable competitive spirit, superior decision making, and a genuine caring for others.

I recall one of the most powerful leadership lessons that I ever learned while I was the COO of Korn/Ferry and on track to become the CEO: that leadership is all about the other person. No matter the topic—whether someone is being fired or has just told you about a serious health issue—that person should leave your office feeling better than when he or she entered.

As the leader it is not just what you say, but what you don't say. As the old adage goes, "Actions speak louder than words," and nowhere is that truer than in the executive office. Everything that a leader says and does sends a message. Words can destroy even the most noble of actions. As I've learned personally over the years, being a leader sometimes means biting your tongue, for example, choosing not to respond to an angry e-mail right away, knowing it's often better to wait. For the CEO there is no off-the-cuff remark. Leadership demands introspection and an understanding of the clout that one's words and actions carry.

As the team comes together, roles, responsibilities, and authority need to cascade down from leader to followers along with a clear picture of how each part relates to the broader vision. As I have seen in my organization, people want and need to know how they are contributing to the journey. When they understand, they will give their all for a chance to be part of something bigger than themselves.

STRATEGY AND PURPOSE

A highly effective tool to develop people is having a vision and mission, which I view as the soul of the organization. Through common purpose, the leader connects with the team, not just intellectually but emotionally. Employees feel that "we're all in this together" because the leader has communicated the vision with passion, openly shared the challenges and opportunities that are anticipated, listened to their feedback, and laid out a course they will navigate together. This connection is vital for organizations today in order to tap the creative potential of all people at all levels.

Certainly companies are in the business of making profits. Although money does provide security and material rewards, it alone is not a sustaining motivator. Far more powerful is the sense of being part of a bigger purpose, for example, how the organization contributes to society and the purpose for which it exists. When an organization is anchored in common purpose, its vision and mission become a rallying cry.

Great leaders know how to marry strategy with purpose. In that way, when the company reaches its business objectives and goals, it can also serve the greater good. For example, as CEO of PepsiCo, Indra Nooyi leads her team of 285,000 employees to achieve "Performance with Purpose": generating sustainable growth while being a positive force in the countries in which PepsiCo operates.

It is not enough for leaders to set forth specific goals; they must also know how to pursue them. Even as they set off on the path toward the desired end point, they need back-up plans—alternative routes, if you will—that allow them to move forward fearlessly and confidently. This is the heart of strategy: how the mission or vision is accomplished.

Edward Miller, a Korn/Ferry board member and former CEO of AXA Financial Inc., once asked me rhetorically whether it was better to have a strategy that is 100-percent perfect but only 75-percent executable or a strategy that is 75-percent perfect but 100-percent executable. Miller concluded that the latter is better, and I wholeheartedly agree.

In order to help others to embrace the strategy and values of the organization, leaders must communicate openly and with a great deal of transparency. Yet leaders cannot stop there. They must also live the strategies and values of the organization. In other words, leaders must be the message. In order for this to happen, leaders must be authentic, humble, and accessible.

Former Mexican president Fox occupied the world stage for the six years of his presidency. Rather than allowing the power and prestige of the office to separate him from others, Fox remained in touch with people to make sure their needs were met. "We closed the office and went out into the field just to make sure things were happening," he explained.

Although many great leaders have charisma, they never let their personalities and egos get in the way. They know they represent something bigger than themselves: their institutions and their positions. Their titles reflect a high level of accomplishment, yet it is not about them; what they do is not who they are. They lead with grace, acknowledging that they are the steward or trustee of whatever organization they represent.

Monitoring and Measuring

A leader has to see not only the big picture but also what is in focus in the here and now. The outcome today will determine the starting point for tomorrow. Just as a driver glances at the dashboard or a pilot watches the instrument panel, the leader monitors and measures continually to know what is going on at all times, particularly regarding competitors. Monitoring and measuring also reflect the personal mission of leaders to continually better themselves. They are curious and engaged and always on the lookout for opportunity. Leaders are intent on learning from every experience, no matter what the outcome is.

They are, in short, lifelong learners whose curiosity and learning agility are formidable assets. Learning agility allows leaders to practice adjustive leadership—adjusting by selecting from within their portfolio of styles and skills what's needed to effectively meet each new situation. Additionally, they have to be able to manage change. Measuring and monitoring also enhance a leader's ability to execute by defining and refining the best ways to get things done. A leader needs to have a sense of how to organize, structure, and process.

Carlos Slim, who ranks number one on the *Forbes* list of billionaires, has the intellect of a scholar and the analytical ability of a mathematician. Since boyhood, when he learned from his father how to keep a balance sheet, Slim has valued measurement and metrics. Measuring and monitoring have allowed him to take on the risks (and the possibility of failure) to be a buyer when others are panicking and selling. He followed the footsteps of his father, who invested during the Mexican Revolution and again after the 1929 stock market crash. Slim found opportunity during Mexico's economic downturn of the 1980s and then after the global financial crisis of 2008–2009.

As a CEO, I know the lessons learned extend beyond the business to myself. To be a leader, I must commit to honesty on a deep level. It starts with being honest with myself, knowing what I do well and where I can challenge myself to stretch, grow, and learn more. The only way to earn the trust and respect of others is to allow them to see who I am as a person. Such transparency is uncomfortable at times, particularly for a private person, and yet it comes with the job. Whether I'm in a meeting with my senior team, giving a speech at a forum, or coaching my son's Little League baseball team, I am the same person. Any inconsistency will erode the trust that I must earn from others. If there are gaps between what I say and what I do, then my words become worthless.

Honesty, of course, goes both ways. A big frustration for any leader is others' reluctance to tell the truth instead of what they think the boss wants to hear. The fact is that people are often afraid to speak up because of the consequences, whether real or perceived. Without a sense of economic and employment security, there is no real "freedom of speech." The challenge for me, as a leader, is to make sure that it is safe for people to tell me the truth, to ascertain if I am in any way contributing toward their reticence to speak freely. If I want the truth, I have to welcome and invite it and give back in kind.

EMPOWERING AND INSPIRING

Empowering and inspiring others is the very essence of leadership. It distinguishes leaders from managers. Managing is essentially making sure that others do what they were asked to do; it is prescriptive and directive and ordinary in execution. Leadership, however, is inspirational and nothing less than extraordinary. Warren Bennis, an author and expert in the field of leadership, wrote, "The manager asks how and when, the leader asks what and why; the manager accepts the status quo, the leader challenges it."[3] A manager plans, organizes, and coordinates. The leader inspires and motivates.

As CEO, Anne Mulcahy faced the enormous task of turning around Xerox, which in 2001 was in turmoil and not expected to survive. As Mulcahy launched a restructuring plan to save Xerox, she communicated honestly and continually with employees, letting them know the severity of the challenges faced and also giving them realistic hope. It was a difficult balancing act and one that was extremely personal for Mulcahy, who had started working at Xerox as a sales rep in 1976. "There wasn't a moment that wasn't intensely focused on making sure the place survived," she recalled.

When leaders truly believe in the abilities of their team, the results can be amazing. People stretch themselves, moving past their own fear of failing, and accomplish more than they thought possible.

For the leader, this does not mean just talking (as in doing all the talking), it also means listening—a lot. When Drew Gilpin Faust became president of Harvard University, she used her well-developed listening skills to reach out to faculty and staff across the university, strengthening her ties with those who already knew her and establishing connections with those who did not. With an open-door policy at her office, Faust welcomed a steady stream of people who came by to share their thoughts, ideas, and concerns, especially with regard to what they saw as critical to the future of the university.

I believe for every leader it is critical to listen and learn first and then to lead. As a CEO, I have become more comfortable with pauses and silence, asking a question and letting it hang in the air a moment before someone answers. With the leaders profiled in this book, after I poked and prodded with my questions a bit, my silence and willingness to listen allowed them to be open and candid. My experience led me to consider an important question regarding the value of silence and listening: what valuable information or intelligence might we as leaders gather if we talked less and listened patiently more?

Reward and Celebrate

As it all comes together—the team, the purpose, the strategy—leaders must remember to take the last and, in some ways, the most important step: reward and celebrate. Leaders cannot take this final step for granted, believing that the annual report or the company newsletter will convey the goals reached, the milestones achieved. Rewarding and celebrating at every step along the way creates loyalty, inspires followers, encourages creativity, and enhances performance to create future successes.

We are all in this together, learning from mistakes and pressing on to the next victory. We are not afraid to fail because we know that there is no real end point until the last one. We are courageous and committed, not only to an outcome, but also to a process of becoming better as organizations, as individuals, and most certainly as leaders.

In the upcoming chapters, I hope you will find both inspiration and information from those who have walked the walk and have graciously shared the lessons learned from every step of the way. Their experiences and examples show how to develop the necessary courage to stretch yourself and take calculated risks, to inspire yourself and others to move beyond what you think is possible—or even probable—to envision a future that is of your making. They will show you how to face the uncertainties and move forward with no fear of failure.

My job is to recruit, attract, and compensate people; provide a moral compass; match their skill sets to different needs in the organization . . . ; and then to make sure that they work collaboratively and collectively.

—Michael Bloomberg, mayor, New York;
founder, Bloomberg LP

Chapter One

MICHAEL BLOOMBERG: EMPOWER

Michael Bloomberg has torn down the walls of city hall—figuratively, that is. Instead of occupying the corner office that housed his predecessors, the 108th mayor of New York sat at a desk much like any other in a huge room known as The Bullpen. The only element distinguishing his desk from the others was the two Bloomberg computer terminals providing live news and market updates—reminders of the namesake company founded by this former Wall Street executive turned philanthropist and politician. All around him, desks were clustered together in a hive of activity that resembled a trading room in look, feel, and intensity.

"I can't think of anything that keeps people from working together as much as a wall," Bloomberg remarked as he looked out over the open room.

The Bullpen seemed a fitting symbol of Bloomberg's leadership, setting the tone for what he does by empowering others. During his long and varied career, Bloomberg has also empowered himself as a leader through his courage to make and stand by tough decisions and the ability to move beyond setbacks and never look back. It is these qualities that attract followers today.

The openness and transparency Bloomberg espouses as a leader were clearly evident throughout the historic city hall in lower Manhattan. The corner office occupied by previous mayors has been turned into an historic tribute, not to any particular person (although the furnishings used by former mayor Rudy Giuliani were still in place), but to the position.

As a leader Bloomberg has taken risks to do things differently, shaking up the status quo with a business imprint of how he runs city government. "The first time I put people in The Bullpen you would have thought the world was coming to an end. Nobody gives me grief about that anymore," he said with a smirk.

Although Bloomberg does keep his hands on the wheel, the gears that move the city churn with the efforts and ideas of others. His leadership style can be summed up in one statement: he empowers and delegates. "You couldn't [recruit] half of these people [to come] here or anywhere else if you didn't delegate," Bloomberg said matter-of-factly.

It seemed only natural to delegate responsibility and authority in order to run a city of 8.3 million people with 300,000 employees and an infrastructure that operates 24/7—just as it would to run a multi-billion-dollar company. Yet, in some organizations, delegation is limited. Information, power, access, and control are held tightly within a very small circle, which is neither particularly effective nor empowering. In governments, power tends to be centralized, a style of management that Bloomberg considered to be the sign of a "control freak." To his way of thinking, in both business and government, delegating is "a very big deal"—engendering mutual trust and igniting passion to achieve a bigger purpose.

"You only get good people if you give them authority. Why would people who are any good want to go to an organization where they are going to be a clerk? You want to be able to do new things," he added. "That doesn't mean I'm always going to accept someone's ideas, but that person has to know he's part of it; otherwise, he doesn't want to work here."

Bloomberg gave the example of recruiting three senior people to serve as deputy mayors in his administration. Any of them would be welcomed—and well compensated—in the private sector, yet they chose to work for the city as part of Bloomberg's team. Instead of financial remuneration, they were motivated by a sense of mission and a desire to make a difference; what they asked for in return was respect and recognition. "Why would any of these three want to come to work for me in a junior position? It's because they want to be part of a team—and I delegate. Delegation is empowering people to make decisions and then backing them," he explained.

During our discussion, it was easy to see why people want to work for Bloomberg: he was accessible and real. No matter that he is mayor of one of the world's most important financial and commercial hubs, that his name has been floated occasionally as a possible presidential candidate, or that he is a successful billionaire entrepreneur, Bloomberg came across as an in-his-shirt-sleeves kind of a guy who brushed off an attempt to address him as Mr. Mayor and insisted on being called Mike. As a leader, Bloomberg was clearly in the trenches with his team.

"My job is to recruit, attract, and compensate people; provide a moral compass; match their skill sets to different needs in the organization that I'm running, whether it's a company or a government; and then to make sure that they work collaboratively and collectively," Bloomberg said. "Find problems before they get out of hand and give people advice."

NEVER LOOK BACK

Asked to describe the key to his success, Bloomberg quickly answered "hard work," which he attributed to his background of growing up in a middle-class family in Massachusetts. He told several stories that exhibited his old-fashioned work ethic of going in early and staying late. For example, between his first and second years at Harvard Business School, Bloomberg had a formative experience while working for a small real estate company whose main business was renting apartments. The company ran generic ads for one-, two-, and three-bedroom apartments, and when people would call, appointments would be set up to show them what was available.

"I would go in at seven in the morning. The phone would ring off the hook. I would talk to everybody, and I'd schedule appointments with them. Then all day long, everyone who came in the door had an appointment to see Michael Bloomberg. I was just a kid. The other four desks were occupied by four adults, and for them, this was their career. They didn't come in until nine o'clock. And they could never figure out why I had all the appointments," Bloomberg said, shaking his head. "All you had to do was come in early! I made enough money to pay for room, board, and tuition for my whole second year at business school that one summer. And it was just showing up and doing the hard work."

The same work ethic made a name for him at Salomon Brothers on Wall Street, which he joined in 1966 right after graduating from Harvard Business School. His habit of being "the first guy in every morning and the last guy out at night" attracted the attention of the number one and number two executives at the firm who became his mentors. Moral of the story, Bloomberg said, "You've got to be there."

Although his early experiences at Salomon honed his work style, being let go by the firm set the tone of his leadership style as an entrepreneur and later as a politician—decisiveness and never looking back. In 1981, Salomon Brothers was acquired and Bloomberg was asked to leave the firm. "Number one, it was time to go. I had talked about leaving a year earlier, and they convinced me to stick around," he recalled. "Then they said, 'Time to go,' and I said fine. I'm sure that for five minutes on the drive back home I probably said, 'Those SOBs,' and that's the last time I thought about it."

The man who said he "never had a bad day other than the day my father died" was hardly sidelined by the career interruption.

Rather than becoming stuck in the past, Bloomberg moved on with the germ of an idea for creating an information company that would bring greater transparency and efficiency to the financial markets. The result was Bloomberg LP. Nearly twenty years after its creation, as of 2010 the company said it had 285,000 subscribers to its financial news and information services in more than one hundred and sixty countries, and eleven thousand employees worldwide. (And as for the executives back at Salomon Brothers who had let him go, "they all became paying customers," Bloomberg added with a laugh.)

With a personal fortune estimated by *Forbes* magazine of $18 billion, ranking him number twenty-three on the list of billionaires for 2010, Bloomberg has been active in philanthropy for years. He supports a variety of causes, including a pediatric hospital at Johns Hopkins named for his mother: the Charlotte R. Bloomberg Children's Center.

In 2001, after years of involvement in civic causes, Bloomberg entered politics, running for mayor and being elected just two months after the September 11 attack on the World Trade Center, the biggest terrorism attack to occur on American soil. He took over the reins from the immensely popular Rudolph Giuliani, who had completed two four-year terms. Bloomberg's political agenda included crime reduction, economic recovery, and turning around the New York City Public Schools. Regarding the last goal, since Bloomberg took office, graduation rates have increased by more than 20 percent and reading and math scores have both risen to record levels.[1]

In his professional, philanthropic, and political endeavors, Bloomberg gave the distinct impression of being a hardworking, determined leader who also has been driven by intellectual curiosity, who once he puts his mind to something will tenaciously pursue it to completion, whether it is the launch of a business or revamping how government operates.

FACING CRITICISM WITHOUT FEAR

Being an elected official, particularly one as visible as Bloomberg, is no easy feat and certainly presents the possibility of failure on occasion, along with dissection and discussion in the press of what could or should be done. Bloomberg clearly has the courage to make the tough decisions, even though he may face criticism at times, and to stand by them. He spoke frankly about what his critics in the press and elsewhere were likely to say if he were to reduce the police department by five thousand officers in 2010 because of budget constraints, or if the number of firefighters on an engine were reduced to five from six as a punitive measure specified in the union contract in response to excessive absenteeism. "You just have to understand that you're going to be vilified for some of these things," he said stoically.

Criticism does not keep Bloomberg away from the battles, including a national brouhaha in early fall 2010 over plans to build an Islamic center that contains a mosque near the site of the World Trade Center. Critics have called the mosque an affront to the families who lost loved ones in the terrorist attacks on the Twin Towers. Proponents have cited freedom of religion as guaranteed by the Bill of Rights. Bloomberg has been a staunch and unwavering supporter of the plan, apparently unfazed by the possibility that his view could be unpopular with some people. It is far better, he believed, to take a stand than to be on the sidelines and silent on an important issue.

Bloomberg has also continued his campaign to raise performance in the city's schools, which sometimes puts him in the crosshairs of controversy. He recounted a recent news article that stated he had lost a court decision on technicalities over closing nineteen schools. The notion that he was somehow the one who lost or failed was clearly irksome to the mayor—after all, these schools have a record of graduating only 10 percent of their students. Who, then, were the losers? To Bloomberg's way of thinking, the students who will face "one more year of getting a bad education" stood to lose the most. "It's the kids who fail, but that's not the way the press writes it," he lamented.

Undeterred, the Bloomberg administration will go back at it again, this time "dotting the i's and crossing the t's" as it pursues the legal process to close the schools. Bloomberg's tenacity on the issue was not about being right but about doing what he felt was right for the students and the school system.

In his sometimes contentious dealings with the press, Bloomberg has drawn a tough line on what he does and does not have to disclose—such as his personal schedule and events that are not public forums. "The first time I said to *The New York Times* that my personal life is my personal life, and unless it is a public event we're not going to disclose it, there was an editorial on how outrageous this was, that they had a right to know everything I did and where I was," Bloomberg said. "Well, if that's the case, you'll never attract anybody to take the job."

His stance was understandable, particularly given the harshness of the spotlight that is on him as a national public figure. Yet, inevitably, all elected officials and many corporate CEOs experience a blurring of the line between their personal and public lives. For some, there appears to be no distinction at all, and they have a feeling that everything about their lives—what they say and do—is public. Living under the microscope, as it were, comes with the territory. Bloomberg, however, believes that a basic level of personal privacy is important, or else many talented leaders will decline to run for office.

Aware that the public watches what he does, Bloomberg said he tries to lead by example, such as by taking the subway every day. "If I am going to ask you to take the subway, why won't I? It is the quickest way to get to work, and it sets an example. Generally speaking, I don't ask anyone to do anything that I don't do."

COMMONALITIES OF THREE WORLDS

From working at the trading desks of Salomon Brothers to becoming a highly successful entrepreneur and then entering politics, Bloomberg made his mark in three very different arenas. And yet Bloomberg saw more commonalities than differences among them, which has enabled him to apply the lessons learned in one area to another. "I think all three of those worlds think that the other two worlds are very different and easy to operate in, and that their one world is the toughest. My experience is that they are all tough. There is no easy answer to complex problems. The commonality is that all have human beings working in them."

With a view that "leadership is leadership" no matter where it is practiced, Bloomberg dismissed the notion of his career path as "that big of a jump from one world to another." After all, the requisites are many of the same skills, such as recruiting and developing a team, managing, handling interpersonal relationships, and using technology. "The problem is convincing people in the new world that you're entering for the first time, because they are so enamored with or know only their own world, so how can you be an outsider and come in and know anything about their world," he explained.

The only distinction he made was in pay for performance, which is prevalent in the private sector, whereas in the public sector compensation and promotions are often subject to civil service laws and union contracts. "The unions make those worlds somewhat different, although I am not one of those believers that the unions are the biggest problem that we have. As a matter of fact, I would argue that the biggest problem we have is the elected officials who over the years have given the unions everything they asked for and put us in an untenable situation," he noted.

Bloomberg drew a parallel to instances in which some corporate executives were criticized for receiving bloated compensation packages, but he thinks the fault lies with the board's compensation committee that approved them. The issue for him was one of accountability.

Given his array of leadership experiences, Bloomberg has an interesting perspective, which he attributed mostly to the fact that he has been around for a while. "You learn with time that the world is complex," he reflected. "To the young whippersnapper, everything looks possible. I still think that everything is possible, but I understand that it might take a little longer to get there."

Under the heading of "lessons learned with time" is having a sense of whether someone would be good in a particular position, which Bloomberg attributed to instinct. "I haven't made very many mistakes either in my company or here [at city hall] in terms of picking people. Some, maybe, you could have done better, but you pick from the people who were available. But with very few did I ever say to myself, 'I made a mistake.'"

When screening candidates, Bloomberg said, he pays no attention to such things as where someone went to school. To prove his point, he called aside a member of his team and asked, "How old are you?" When the staff member answered, "thirty-five," Bloomberg launched into a rhetorical argument on why it should not matter from which college the man had graduated thirteen years before. "There is value to formal education, but leadership is about people, and people are subjective," Bloomberg continued.

He recalled a lecture he has given to college students on seeking a job. The typical approach taken by young graduates, he explained, is to find out about the company and then tell the interviewer what they've learned. "That's not what the guy on the other side of the desk wants to hear. The interviewer has a job: that is to find good people. You've got to tell him what you can do, not why you want the job. And to go in and say that you know enough to run the company; in my mind, I just disqualify any young person who does that. I understand when someone says, 'I'm a hard worker and I want to learn, and everybody says it's a great place to work.' But you can't say you know all the answers."

When he interviews judges who are up for reappointment to civil, criminal, and family court positions, Bloomberg said, he is far less interested in the answers (the questions he asks are often purposefully ambiguous) than he is in whether the person can take a position and defend it.

"I ask questions for which there is no right or wrong answer," Bloomberg explained. "Here's one: a judge has to decide whether to take a kid away from the parents and send him to foster care. It's the parents' kid, and the situation is not life threatening. How good is the foster parent going to be? There is no right answer, and every once in a while you are going to have a tragedy when someone gets killed and you could have done the opposite. Why do you make one decision versus another? It's called instinct and judgment—and it's a nonquantifiable thing."

Bloomberg said he is not even particularly interested in judges' records of being liberal or conservative, whether they have the tendency to incarcerate or send people to a halfway house, or if they hold views on politics or social philosophy that are congruent with his. "Those are not the criteria I look for," he added. "The criteria I look for are integrity, intelligence, and a rational basis for making decisions. Could a rational person, given a series of facts that we are discussing, come up with a decision? That's the test."

For business leaders looking to hire team members, Bloomberg's approach of picking people less on the basis of where they have been and more because of who they are and how they make decisions is worth examining. Our work at Korn/Ferry has shown that people who are able to stay receptive and flexible do best in very complex and demanding leadership roles. These are the people who can successfully navigate new situations, who are sufficiently attuned to social nuance and complexity and can consider diverse data in their planning and execution. One of the biggest problems in up-and-coming leaders is rigidity. Those who lack agility to adapt and learn will fail. However, those who can deal with ambiguity, uncertainty, diversity, paradox, novelty, and social complexity will most likely fare better in the long run.

Bloomberg also had advice for managers who need to fire someone, which can be one of the most uncomfortable interactions in the workplace. "The first time someone does something [wrong], have a conversation. I'm very open. People have to trust me, and I have to trust them," he said. However, if being fired comes as a total surprise to the employee, Bloomberg called it inexcusable. "If they never saw it coming, you're just not a good manager."

Leadership Is in the Results

Decisiveness was clearly an attribute that Bloomberg valued in himself and others. "I never second-guess," he said, demonstrating the fact that leaders need to be able to live with their decisions and take accountability for the results. "The difference between being pigheaded and having the courage of your convictions is only in your results," he explained. "It's the same process, but you have to give it some time."

His remark brought home the point that the true measure of leadership is the execution, with how well objectives and goals are pursued, plans are implemented, and results are realized. At times, the leader will need to stay the course; at others, a change becomes necessary. It takes experience and instinct to know the difference.

"When I make a decision, every once in a while someone will say, 'That was a stupid decision,' and, yeah, every once in a while you change your mind overnight. The tougher the decision, though, the longer you have to stick with it, unless it turns out you were really wrong." The art of leadership is to know the difference: when it's time to make a quick turn and when you need to give things a chance to play out. That discernment can only come from having the experience—including having made some bad judgments.

"You've got to be able to analyze it and say, 'I might have gone in a different direction,'" Bloomberg said as a wry smile spread across his face. "But never let the bastards see that they can beat you."

In what seemed to be as fast as a New York minute, Bloomberg said good-bye and went off to the next meeting: the mayor on the move across The Bullpen, where the hum of the city could clearly be heard.

I've always been a risk taker. But I've always been able to look at the downside and never bet the farm. We've done things that haven't worked out, but we've had a lot more winners than losers.

—Eli Broad, venture philanthropist,
The Broad Foundations;
cofounder, Kaufman & Broad (KB Home);
founder, SunAmerica

Chapter Two

Eli Broad: Competitor

By any measure, Eli Broad is a winner with an impressive list of accomplishments. One of the cofounders of Kaufman & Broad, he grew the business from a tract of houses built in the 1950s to a national, publicly traded homebuilding company eventually known as KB Home. Later, he bought a small life insurance company for $65 million and turned that into SunAmerica, a retirement savings empire that was sold in 1999 for $18 billion. A self-made billionaire on the *Forbes* list, he no longer leads the two Fortune 500 companies he founded but remains very active as a venture philanthropist; rather than writing checks and staying at arm's length, he wants to see the results of where he puts his money. The Broad Foundations—which he cofounded with his wife, Edythe—have been a catalyst for change in many areas. With assets of $2.1 billion, the foundations focus on education reform, scientific and medical research, and the arts.

During my twenty-five years working in Los Angeles, I had never met Broad (his last name rhymes with *road*) before, although his reputation had preceded him, as well as his supposed tough "my way or the highway" persona as a demanding, results-driven boss who expected people to follow him unquestioningly. On meeting him in person, I discovered my preconceptions were unfounded. As we began talking, I could see the toughness he was known for, evident mostly in his sense of purpose. More striking was how humble and authentic he was. Broad has not forgotten his modest background as the son of immigrants and, like most of the leaders interviewed for this book, exhibited a work ethic that harkens back to earlier and leaner times.

At seventy-seven years of age, Broad has high energy and curiosity. An avid learner, he spoke of reading four newspapers a day—always on the lookout for ideas, inspiration, or a new approach. Like any enlightened leader, Broad has an insatiable appetite for learning and information.

Just by looking at his desk, I could see how engaged and involved Broad still was. His desk was stacked high with papers, each pile representing one of his many areas of interest, from reforming K–12 education in urban areas to genomic research to supporting public access to and appreciation of contemporary art. "I'm not one who has a clean desk," he chuckled. "Every stack has a purpose."

As we talked, it was clear that problems and challenges were also stacked up in his quick mind, among them America's competitiveness in the global economy. Rather than dwelling on the past, including his own accomplishments, Broad spoke with urgency about the current state of business today in America. A competitive leader, he was intent on sharing his perspective and knowledge of the playing field so that others can also compete more effectively and win.

THE GLOBAL COMPETITIVE VIEW

As Broad described it, emerging markets are gaining, and the United States is falling behind in a particularly critical area: education. "I am worried about this country. Education is where it starts in my view. We used to be number one in [the high school graduation rate among developed countries]; now we are number eighteen. We read in the national press how poorly our kids are doing: a 50 percent graduation rate in most urban areas. In Detroit [where Broad grew up] it is 28 percent," he observed. "Unless we do better, we are in deep trouble compared to what is happening in Korea, Japan, India, China, and some other countries. Look at their trajectory versus ours and you know they are going to come out ahead of us."

Broad reflected on the considerable challenges faced by CEOs today. He fretted over persistently high unemployment in the United States that could hover around 8 percent or higher through 2011 and a "real" unemployment rate (counting those who are underemployed and still looking for jobs as well as those who have given up) that was estimated at 17 percent. The loss of jobs across every industry and sector made him wonder where job growth would emerge in the future. With healthcare reform becoming a reality at the time of our conversation in spring 2010, Broad declared that a healthcare system that accounted for 16.5 percent of gross domestic product (GDP) and was on track to grow to 18 to 20 percent was one that the United States couldn't afford. The economy has needed a considerable amount of stimulus, which not only will eventually go away, but also will almost certainly be replaced with higher taxes. The engine that propels the American economy has been consumers who reached into an artificial piggy bank created by easy credit to fund conspicuous consumption.

"The country has a lot of problems. How are we going to get out of it? I do not see a clear path. This is a great country. We've got great innovation and so on, but we haven't done well in other areas," Broad commented.

Looking ahead through 2011 to 2012 and beyond, signals were mixed; some indications suggested that a corner had been turned, and others looked for low growth ahead. Broad echoed the uncertainty. "I don't know what the engine is going to be that will get us out of it. Look at the number of jobs we've lost. What are we going to replace them with? Hopefully, things in the energy sector, but that's going to be slow."

Broad is a realist but certainly not a pessimist. In our conversation, he related glimmers of hope and signs of progress. His advice for CEOs was to be cautious and avoid being overly aggressive while making moves strategically, particularly in emerging markets. "Look at the growth rates of China, India, Korea, and elsewhere—how quickly their universities are improving, how productive they can be," he added. "The large multinationals, whether American based or European based, have a big advantage over just domestic companies."

His comments demonstrated that if CEOs were aware of the variables on the macro and micro levels, they would be better able to anticipate what they are likely to face and respond proactively, especially in advance of their competitors. Broad, however, has never focused too much on the long term. Whether speaking to CEOs or college graduates, he gives the same time frame for making plans and charting changes: never look beyond five years. "I don't believe in twenty-year plans. You want to be out there two to five years and visualize what can be achieved rather than think out too far in the future when there are too many things that can happen. The world changes very rapidly," he explained.

Looking at the world at large, Broad equated competitiveness with strong leadership in all sectors—in corporations, state and federal governments, and school districts around the country. To him, that meant leaders who are willing to tackle the difficult, unpopular issues, whether it's dealing with unfunded pensions for public employees and retiree health benefits or promoting exports to bolster the U.S. economy. "The way forward is to have tough leadership that's willing to do things," he said.

Broad gave one example of a leader he admires: New York City mayor Michael Bloomberg whose city administration has managed to ban smoking in public places and trans fats in the city's restaurants. "He did a lot of things that people said couldn't be done," Broad said. That praise could just as easily be applied to Broad, from his days as an innovative homebuilder to his venture philanthropy of today.

The Importance of a Winning Record

Broad is famous for being a tough competitor, one who always wants to win—and that word frequently punctuated our discussion on leadership. In our hour-long conversation, Broad mentioned *winning* and *losing* (or words such as *success* or *failure*) a total of twenty times. Intriguingly, for such a driven competitor, he neither fears losing—which he sees as inevitable on occasion—nor lets it get in his way. "I've always been a risk taker. But I've always been able to look at the downside and never bet the farm. We've done some things that haven't worked out, but we've had a lot more winners than losers." Broad was clearly at peace with the possibility of failure as long as he maintained an overall winning record. By racking up victories, leaders attract others to their missions, which will help them accomplish the hard work that needs to be done.

"I define leadership as the ability to have other people follow you and work with you. A leader comes in various forms. There is no one model for a leader. There are some who are so charismatic, that gets the job done. Others are not charismatic, but they are respected. There are others who are not only respected but also are viewed as winners so people want to be with them and engaged with them," Broad observed. "I'm not sure leaders are born. I don't think I was born a leader. I think I became a leader, not because of my personality or charm but because I work very hard at it. People respected that. I accomplished a lot of things. They saw me as someone who was a winner, so to speak, and they wanted to be part of the organization that I created, whether it was in homebuilding with KB Home, formerly Kaufman & Broad, or with SunAmerica, and the same thing is true in philanthropy. We've got a lot of very bright people here at The Broad Foundations. They believe in the mission.

They believe in the success that we've had and hopefully will continue to have."

With his talk of winning and losing, Broad sounded a bit like a coach who cajoles and inspires his team to victory, but he would not take the analogy further than that. "If you're a CEO and you have great people who are very bright and very challenging, you can't inspire them the way you can an athletic team, whether it's before the game or at half-time. You do some of that," he said. "But it's also about having a clear mission that the team believes can be accomplished. They need a leader who has won a lot of games in the past, and they want to be on that team."

When I asked him hypothetically about a new leader who does not have a track record as yet, Broad conceded that the team will give the leader a chance but only for so long. "He better start winning!" he added. "Look, unless they have to, people will not stick with a loser. If you want to get the best and brightest people, they are going to want to be with someone who is a winner."

In order to win, leaders need a mission, a common purpose around which others can rally. The role of the leader is to convince people that the goal is achievable, no matter how lofty, distant, or difficult. "Part of the job of a leader is to get people to do more than they thought they could do," Broad added.

As a leader, Broad is genuinely interested in the development of people. The ideal team for him is composed of bright, capable individuals who are willing to challenge his thinking with their own ideas. He'd rather receive input on how something might be done better than fill the ranks with people who only say yes. In short, he wants a winning team: a community of like-minded individuals to pursue the projects about which he is most passionate in order to change the world—or at least mold it a bit to his vision.

Broad's eye for talent seeks out people who display a lot of potential, even if they don't have a lengthy track record. "First of all, you look at someone's resume. Where did they come from? What kind of education did they have? What have they accomplished? How smart are they? You ask a lot of questions, talk about their last few positions—what worked for them and what didn't. What were they unhappy about? I have also found that most of the people you want are not looking for a job."

Broad clearly derived a sense of pride from developing others to the point of changing their lives, such as the direct reports in his companies who later went on to become CEOs at other firms. "I feel good about finding people and seeing them progress, pushing them to achieve things they were not sure they could do," he said. "I try to set an example: I never ask people to do anything I wasn't willing to do."

FROM HUMBLE ROOTS TO GREAT ACCOMPLISHMENTS

Broad spoke with the confidence of a person who had set high goals for himself, then achieved and surpassed them. His roots are humble. His parents were Lithuanian immigrants; his mother was a dressmaker, and his father started out as a housepainter and later owned two five-and-dime stores. Broad admitted he did not do well in high school but excelled in college. "I like to question everything. High school teachers didn't like that. College professors love students who do that," he explained with a smile.

At Michigan State, he majored in accounting and minored in economics and graduated in three years. Just a few weeks shy of his twenty-first birthday, he became the youngest person in the state of Michigan to take and pass the Certified Public Accountant examination. After working for two years as an accountant making $67.40 a week after taxes, he decided to start his own business. The homebuilders for whom he did tax preparation were making a lot more money than he was, and they probably weren't as smart. Rather than imitate, Broad decided to innovate.

With $25,000 borrowed from his in-laws, Broad cofounded with Donald Kaufman (his wife's cousin's husband) a home-building company. The idea was to build houses without basements, which was being done elsewhere but was unheard of at the time in Detroit. As far as Broad was concerned, basements were only a holdover from the days when houses used coal for heat; doing away with them would keep the price point down. Then, he could offer what homeowners really wanted, which were carports.

"We came up with a product. Everybody said, 'No one will buy it,'" he remembered. The houses, priced at $13,740, went on sale in January 1957. They sold out the first weekend. Kaufman & Broad was officially launched. A year and a half later, twenty-six-year-old Eli Broad became a millionaire.

"When we started, life was very simple. If you built a home and the monthly payments even before tax benefits were equal to or less than rent, people would buy," Broad explained. By the time Broad was twenty-eight years old, Kaufman & Broad Building Company (which later became KB Home) went public, the first homebuilder to be listed on the New York Stock Exchange. In 1971, Kaufman & Broad bought Sun Life Insurance, which was then a traditional life insurance company. After deciding that people were more interested in having money to retire with than death benefits, he repositioned the company in the early 1990s as SunAmerica with a line of retirement investment products. Changing Sun Life into SunAmerica was a calculated risk, and some of the things the company did reflected that same entrepreneurial spirit—like investing in national advertising to create a brand, which was labeled as foolishness and a waste of money by others. "We did a lot of things differently," Broad said, a hint of pride in his voice.

His success has stemmed at least in part from his ability to evaluate risks but never to take on too much. "I knew there were risks—risk of failure, that we wouldn't accomplish it. I'd measure the risks versus the reward, and if I thought the odds were in our favor, we'd go ahead and do it," he explained.

CHALLENGING THE LEADER

Although he came across as a firm, in-charge leader, Broad said he is open to input from his team, even to the point of dissent, provided that it is delivered appropriately, which means face-to-face with him or another leader in the organization and not publicly. Anyone who persists in speaking out publicly, whether coming out against management or grumbling that the mission cannot be accomplished (which is a growing concern for companies these days given greater transparency and broader dissemination of thoughts and opinions online), should be shown the door. But challenging the leader with diverse opinions, Broad said, actually strengthens the team.

"You don't want a bunch of robots running around. You want people who have ideas, who are going to challenge you and push you. You want people who are going to say, 'I'm not sure you are doing the right thing. You ought to do it a different way.' You want to listen to all that, but at the end of the day, as they say, the buck stops here. You make a decision, and you expect them to follow it," he added.

For a leader it can be a tremendous burden to shoulder: to look in the mirror and know that whatever decision was made, he or she must live with the consequences, good or bad. That becomes even tougher knowing that no one is right all of the time. Broad accepts the responsibility as part of what it means to be a leader.

As for his reputation for being a tough boss, Broad explained with a laugh, "There's a story around here that you're either here six weeks or you're here for twenty years." His attitude was consistent with his focus on winning: in order to accomplish the stated goals and objectives, the team must be unified by common purpose and committed to carry out the leader's vision. Those who make the grade are rewarded for their accomplishments.

Broad has had a strong hand on the wheel of the companies and organizations he leads. Therefore, it's hard to imagine him being in the CEO role while someone else serves as chairman, a model that some corporate governance advocates suggest for large, publicly traded firms. Yet Broad said he would not have opposed that arrangement. "I've always had strong directors. It would not have bothered me to have a lead director or a chairman as long as I was the CEO," he added. "I want to be challenged. I'm one of those people who ask a lot of questions. You know, when the going gets tough, you need people like this."

Broad believes board members must be more willing than ever to ask tough questions of management, which means becoming more educated about the company, especially its products and services. "The days of the two-hour board meeting and then you go home are over. Board members have got a lot more responsibility today and not only as a result of regulations or law but also in general. Directors have responsibilities beyond even shareholders and employees to the public at large and customers," he said.

FINANCIAL REWARDS

Broad boasted about the two hundred people who worked for KB Home and SunAmerica who became millionaires through ownership of the company stock as share prices rose, which benefited all shareholders. "We had a reputation of not paying as much as others. We believed in ownership—options and the like. So people did well if our shareholders did well. We had a real community of interests," he noted.

Broad believes many CEOs in America are overpaid, but he made a clear distinction between his cash compensation as a CEO and the wealth that he and others in his companies amassed through stock ownership. "If you took my cash compensation, it was never that big. I don't think my salary was ever more than $400,000. I made money because I made it for the shareholders. Our people made money because we made it for the shareholders," he explained.

Speaking of shareholder value, Broad notes that KB Home and SunAmerica produced a better return than even one of the best investors of all time. "If you look at our record, we did better for our shareholders than Warren Buffet did at Berkshire Hathaway in the 1990s," he said. "And I feel good about the products that were being produced, whether homes or retirement savings."

Broad recalled a stock incentive he instituted, which was based on earnings and vested according to how well the company performed compared to the S&P 500. "That incentive paid off in spades for me and for a lot of people," he added.

MOTIVATING OTHERS TO CHANGE

One of the toughest jobs a leader faces is getting people to change. The task is so daunting that when asked how it can be accomplished, Broad shook his head for a moment before answering. "It varies," he said finally and then returned to his favorite example, the education system. He spoke of the frustration of trying to motivate people who are entrenched in the status quo, whether educators, school board members, or administrators. "Sometimes you get them to change by financial means, but that's tough in education. Sometimes you get them to change by public opinion. . . . You get them to change by competition [such as] charter schools and showing how successful they are versus other public schools. Sometimes it comes from the top. Sometimes it's forced by the federal government. . . . There's no simple way."

The lesson for leaders to extrapolate is to find what motivates their teams, whether incentives or a sense of ownership and common purpose. Winning, however, cannot just be about the prize.

Reflecting on his motivation, Broad said it was never about money. Once a certain amount of wealth has been amassed and a lifestyle has been achieved, multiples of that money will not make an appreciable difference. Rather, his drive comes from a combination of curiosity and impatience. "Whenever I get to some level, I never want to stop. I want to know, 'What do we do next, what do we achieve next?' I like to work. I'm driven; I'm competitive. I want the people around me to have those same attributes, to be as crazy as I am," he said.

Such drive to achieve comes at a price, which Broad readily admitted. "You don't spend enough time with your family. You're not the most well-rounded individual in the world. I know very few leaders who have enough time to be on the golf course two or three times a week, to take a nice vacation, and so on."

By the time Broad reached his forties, he began to achieve more of a sense of balance in his life. For that, he credited art and the influence of his wife, Edythe, who years ago began collecting contemporary works. "That's when I said there's more to life than dealing with bankers and other businesspeople. I became interested in the arts."

Having left the world of commerce in 1999, Broad said he works harder now than when he ran two Fortune 500 companies.

Across the span of his career, Broad has exhibited the leadership of a winner: espousing a bold vision, taking calculated risks without fear, and challenging others to achieve more than they thought possible. Looking back, Broad said there were no "magic whispers" in his ear from any one mentor, which he attributed to the fact that he did not join a company and rise through the ranks while being coached and groomed by a CEO.

When it comes to philanthropy, however, Broad was quick to come up with a role model: industrialist Andrew Carnegie, who amassed a fortune and then proceeded to give much of it away. "I've always had admiration for Carnegie, for all he did and especially his philosophy that he who dies with wealth dies in shame."

A strong competitor, Broad has seen the kinds of returns enjoyed by innovators who capitalize on a new opportunity or untapped market. Vision alone is not enough; leaders must also have the courage to put plans into place. Leaders never act alone. They purposefully build and empower teams that are aligned with a common purpose, such as creating products and venturing into new areas that improve the quality of life of consumers. Like the coach of a high-powered team, a competitor leader knows there are bound to be losses and defeats along the way but hopes the wins will outnumber the losses.

[Leadership] is connecting the dots to form a picture when others may know the dots exist, but not that they connect into a picture. Only you see that you have to connect the dots and make the picture emerge.
—Indra Nooyi, chairman and CEO, PepsiCo

Chapter Three

INDRA NOOYI: PURPOSE

PepsiCo's corporate headquarters, situated on 150 landscaped acres in Purchase, New York, still show traces of the original design as a polo ground. The grounds and gardens are open to the public, but there remains an unmistakable air of privilege and prestige.

At the time of our conversation Indra Nooyi had been chairman and CEO of PepsiCo for nearly four years, but she took none of it for granted: not the beautiful setting, not the large corporate campus filled with art, and certainly not the position she occupies. "I have an immigrant mentality, which is that the job can be taken away at any time, so make sure you earn it every day," Nooyi, who was born in India, explained. "When immigrants come here, they have no safety net—zero. I landed here with $500 in my pocket. I had no one here to pay for me."

Nooyi came to the United States in 1978 to pursue a management degree from Yale School of Management, and success soon followed. Today, as CEO of a company with the world's largest food and beverage portfolio, she has broken the corporate sound barrier—flying a little faster and higher than many of her peers. Yet her early experience of being on her own and feeling the need to prove herself never left her. "You always have this fear that you've got to do a great job, that you earn your job that day so you don't get thrown out the next day," she added.

Nooyi is clearly a person of contrasts. Although she is a strategic thinker who values inductive reasoning to anticipate the company's future challenges and opportunities, during our conversation Nooyi also exhibited an emotional, spiritual side. As the head of a corporation with mega-brands such as Pepsi and Frito-Lay, Nooyi keeps a macro focus, and yet her concern for and knowledge of the minutiae of her company's operations are clear.

Given these contrasting approaches, I was eager to find out more about Nooyi's perspective on leadership. In her crisply accented English, she explained in depth the aspects of successful and genuine leadership she has identified over the years and expressed clear views on what leadership was not. Her view was comprehensive, taking in the big picture as well as the small details. She was both thoughtful and challenging at the same time.

"To be honest, I don't know if *leadership* is a word that you would define. I think that leadership is an act, it's a state of mind, it's a behavior," Nooyi said. "To say leadership is doing A or B is trivializing the concept. There are many books written about leadership and even more talk about leadership. But to me, leadership is very personal. It is accomplishing certain objectives that you lay out for yourself and your organization. To define leadership is very, very hard because it's so incredibly complex."

Nooyi soundly dismissed the concept that leadership was as simple as hiring the right people and putting them in place. Her vision of leadership revealed complexities and nuances, which can only be learned on the job and which, as she said, were personal to each leader. "What is leadership? I think leadership is one of the most complex acts that one can perform. It is connecting the dots to form a picture when others may know the dots exist, but not that they connect into a picture. Only you see that you have to connect the dots and make the picture emerge," she explained. "Leadership is having the ability to look around the corner and tell people that something is coming that they absolutely won't accept. Leadership is showing courage in the face of adversity. And it's difficult. Sometimes you want to let yourself relax, but you can't. You have to remain courageous to the whole organization in the face of the worst adversity."

In addition to a leader's outward focus on the organization, Nooyi also emphasized the importance of the internal component to leadership—a personal side. She described this as showing one's vulnerabilities in order to demonstrate "you are a person and not a robot." Calling leadership both "IQ and EQ" (intellectual intelligence and emotional intelligence, respectively), Nooyi reflected on the balancing act required to concentrate on the entire organization while not losing focus on the individual employee. "You must have great empathy for every individual, and at the same time you've got to have a level of abstraction from them so that you don't get too carried away with their individual issues.

"How do you train for this? How do you develop people to think in such a broad way, especially given the current economy? Not easy," Nooyi concluded.

She explained that a successful leader has to narrow the communication gap within the organization. Rather than being distant or aloof, the CEO must purposefully reach out not only to senior executives and direct reports, but also to every employee. Nooyi accomplishes this by writing a letter to all employees every other week on whatever topic is on her mind, from baseball to diversity and inclusion.

Communication is not limited to employees. For years Nooyi has fostered close relationships with the spouses of her executive team and frequently writes them thank-you notes for their support and to acknowledge the burden on the family when an executive travels frequently. Married for thirty years and the mother of two children, ages seventeen and twenty-six, Nooyi knows all too well the family stresses that go along with a busy career. She also lunches with the spouses of the executives on occasion, which forges a loyal connection to the company and allows her to gather market intelligence. "Because I am a woman, I can have lunches with the spouses and we can have great conversations. We've been doing that for years," she said. "They know an awful lot about our business. I ask them for feedback."

Nooyi has extended her personal reach even further by writing to the parents of the executives who work for her. Although the gesture may seem a bit over-the-top, for Nooyi it was both genuine and absolutely required. In letters to the parents of her twenty-nine executive committee members she explained who she was, why she was writing to them, and what their son or daughter was doing for PepsiCo. Most important, she thanked them for the gift of the child they had raised who had become a valuable member of the PepsiCo team. Nooyi credits her parents for her own drive and ambition.

"It [writing the notes] bonded my team closer to the company," she said. "I would encourage every CEO to do this."

Although Nooyi has been tireless when it comes to reaching out to others, communication must go both ways. Listening, she says, is even more important than talking. When CEOs truly listen, they hear ideas on how to solve problems and improve operations and forge better ties with the workforce. Nooyi reads every e-mail that employees send to her. "They want to talk to the CEO. They want to know you are a person. They want to reach out to you," she explained.

Employees also provide what Nooyi calls "tough feedback" at times. She insisted that "they can tell me anything. . . . They tell me things I don't know." Nooyi's experience runs contrary to the usual frustration voiced by other leaders. Most leaders say it is difficult to get employees and subordinates to deliver truthful feedback. To some extent employee reticence is understandable; reliance on someone for your paycheck does not always foster brutal honesty. Yet Nooyi believes her straight-talking approach has overcome this problem. "Some people are more honest than others. Some people think long and hard before they say something to my face or might couch it in nice words. At the end of the day I tell them, 'Is this what you want to tell me? Just say it like it is. Don't try to be polite about it because I can take it.'"

PERFORMANCE WITH PURPOSE

Although internal communication is critical, Nooyi also explained how leadership of a large multinational firm extends well beyond the company's walls. As Nooyi sees it, she must also focus on each individual country in which the organization does business. "Large companies like ours have a duty of caring for every country and every society in which we operate. It's apportioning time to both the company and the country," she added.

Such thinking has led Nooyi to adopt what she calls "Performance with Purpose" as her mission and operating strategy for the company. It is a multipart strategy that lays out country-specific performance targets and detailed goals to benefit society, the environment, and the workforce. Performance with Purpose is Nooyi's passion, and she spoke with obvious pride as she discussed the tenets of this philosophy of doing business: delivering sustainable growth while improving the planet and the health and well-being of people everywhere. It was clear as we spoke that Performance with Purpose is not just a marketing slogan or a tag line. Nooyi is fully committed to this strategy as a means of governing how the company makes, moves, and markets its products with purpose.

With initiatives from more efficient consumption of water and electricity to sustainable farming practices and expanding affordable, nutritional products for lower-income consumers, Performance with Purpose touches every aspect of PepsiCo's businesses. Yet, it is also a highly personal mission for Nooyi. "Because I was born outside the United States, I saw how companies can be both a force for good and a force for bad in emerging markets—multinational companies in particular," she explained. "I saw what they could do to create jobs, bring technology, and improve the quality of life, but also how they could come in and take resources away from the local country. I saw the best and the worst and felt very deeply that, as a CEO, I had to make sure that our company would not operate as if we are an inanimate being. We have to show that we care about every community in which we operate. In every country, I wanted local people to view us as a company that is domiciled in that country—that we are 'local' too. The best way to approach this is to ask, 'How do we, as a company, bring the muscle and the skeleton of this global enterprise and marry it with the wisdom and the soul of each country?'"

PepsiCo has taken Performance with Purpose a step further by committing publicly to all of its goals for both performance and purpose through 2020. These goals were discussed in detail in the 2010 annual report with progress and metrics updated online.

Although many corporate leaders speak about corporate social responsibility, those activities are often ancillary to the company's business. Performance with Purpose as Nooyi envisions it penetrates every aspect of the company's operations. "It is not focusing on performance during the day and doing good deeds on the side. In fact, we have to execute our purpose objectives in order to deliver performance," she added. "It is not Performance *and* Purpose; it is not Performance *or* Purpose; it is Performance *with* Purpose. So every aspect of what we do is driven by the sense of purpose."

When she unveiled Performance with Purpose in 2006, the year she became CEO, it was a challenge to get her team to embrace it. But eventually they did, and it has influenced the corporate culture in a way that even Nooyi finds surprising. She described watching a PBS show one evening about a disabled veteran, Sgt. Eric Edmundson in New Bern, North Carolina, who was being cared for by his parents.

"When I watched that show I was upset beyond . . . ," Nooyi said, her voice breaking with emotion as her words trailed off.

The story hit home in part because New Bern is the birthplace of Pepsi, where Caleb Bradham invented the beverage in his pharmacy in 1898. Nooyi didn't need anything more than that coincidence to propel her into action. She called the local PepsiCo branch manager and asked him to deliver PepsiCo products and coupons to the Edmundsons and to deliver a personal letter that she wrote to the family. But what surprised Nooyi was the PepsiCo manager's response to what was done for the Edmundsons. "He said, 'I am proud to work for a company that delivers on its promise of Performance with Purpose. This is Performance with Purpose at its best,'" Nooyi added. "So when somebody on the front line says that, you know it has permeated through the company."

The Importance of Inductive Thinking

Although Nooyi has touched the soul of PepsiCo, she has not neglected its brain. All purpose with no performance is not sustainable. Nooyi was careful to set specific top- and bottom-line targets for each of the business units. "If we didn't, people would throw me out," she said, displaying the disarming frankness for which she is known.

Nooyi has also changed thinking at the company, favoring inductive over deductive reasoning, which she sees as a key leadership skill. "You almost have to say, 'This is what I think is going to happen so let's talk about what we need to do about this. These are the data points and these are the consequences.' You almost have to force the organization into induced thinking rather than letting them deduce," she explained.

Her emphasis on inductive thinking reminded me of the leadership skill of anticipating. Whether it's a change in the competitive landscape, a new opportunity, or trouble brewing on the macro-economic horizon, leaders must anticipate what is next and act accordingly. Sitting in her book-lined office, Nooyi demonstrated her analytical side and keen mind, characteristics that brought her success in consulting and in operating roles, as she described the need to "look around the corner" to see what is coming.

Nooyi credited experiences early in her career as a strategy consultant with Boston Consulting Group (BCG) for teaching her inductive thinking that helped shape her leadership style. It seemed surprising that Nooyi would cite this phase of her career as being so influential given the fact that a consultant typically develops different skill sets than an operating manager, especially when it comes to such things as inspiring people and running a business. Nooyi was insistent, however. "I don't think I could have gotten here without a strategy consultant background because it taught me inductive thinking. It taught me how to think of the problem in micro terms but also to zoom out and put the problem in the context of its broader environment and then zoom back in to solve the problem. The other thing I learned in strategy consulting is how you can go into an absolutely unknown industry and identify what issues need to be addressed, and then have enough abstraction from the issues to come up with genuine lessons that can be applied. I have learned incredible skills in consulting."

LEARNING TO BE A CEO

As much as Nooyi credited her experience with BCG as "absolutely the best job to go into," it was clear that she viewed strategic consulting as the foundation—not the structure—of her career. "That was more than thirty years ago," she said with a smile that softened only slightly the firmness of the point she was making. "I've been around the bend in corporations."

After BCG, Nooyi worked for Motorola and Asea Brown Boveri and then PepsiCo, which she joined in 1994 as chief strategist—reportedly after turning down an opportunity to work for Jack Welch at General Electric. She quickly made her mark on the company, urging then-CEO Roger Enrico to spin off PepsiCo's fast-food businesses including Taco Bell, Pizza Hut, and KFC in 1997. Other moves she helped orchestrate include the 1998 purchase of Tropicana and a $13 billion merger with Quaker Oats in late 2000.

In 2001, she became president and chief financial officer, which deepened her leadership skills and experiences as well as her knowledge of the company. When she became CEO five years later, however, nothing could quite prepare her for the demands of the job. "The one thing I have learned as a CEO is that leadership at various levels is vastly different. When I was leading a function or a business, there were certain demands and requirements to be a leader. As you move up the organization, the requirements for leading that organization don't grow vertically; they grow exponentially," Nooyi explained. "When I was president of the company, I said, 'Okay, I can do this—piece of cake.' Then when you are the CEO, the responsibilities multiply enormously because you worry about everything."

Her observation applies not only to herself but also to every CEO who discovers this position requires a vastly different array of responsibilities. No matter how close a leader has been to the CEO—serving as CFO, president, or COO—nothing quite compares with being in the top job. In order to succeed, CEOs must not only draw on previous experiences and abilities they have developed, but also commit to lifelong learning as a process of continual self-improvement. The more the leader is willing to expand and grow, the more vibrant the organization will be.

Nooyi related this lesson by quoting what she considers one of the best pieces of advice she ever received: "The distance between number one and number two is always a constant. If you want to improve the organization, you have to improve yourself and the organization gets pulled up with you. That is a big lesson. I cannot just expect the organization to improve if I don't improve myself and lift the organization, because that distance is a constant." Her comment echoed what Korn/Ferry has found in its work: that learning agility is a key predictor of executive success.

A tireless worker who sleeps no more than four or five hours a night, Nooyi shoulders the responsibility that goes along with being CEO to stretch herself while she takes the company forward. "Just because you are CEO, don't think you have landed," she said. "You must continually increase your learning, the way you think, and the way you approach the organization. I've never forgotten that."

Learning and growing as a leader means Nooyi focuses not only on the big picture, but also on the details. She related her experience of doing store checks to see how the company's Pepsi-Cola, Frito-Lay, Quaker, Tropicana, and Gatorade products were displayed in a neighborhood store. "I notice everything. The printing quality—if the printing is bad or if the color is off. If it's a Hispanic store and we don't have enough Hispanic offerings there. Why isn't this merchandised so that the shopper mom can pick things up easily?" With a slightly mischievous smile she added, "I pick up the details that drive the organization insane. But sweating the details is more important than anything else."

BUILDING A TEAM

In spite of her tendency to focus on the smallest details herself, Nooyi's approach to management doesn't preclude delegation and working as a team. She recognizes that she is only as good as the team she brings together. Her job is to knit together strong individual performers into a team that cares first and foremost about the overall organization. "I am blessed with a team that says, 'We've got to worry about PepsiCo,' and they are also fiercely competitive," she said. "Competition makes you thrive. As a company, when you are focusing on something, you do better than when you don't have a target to focus on."

Nooyi attributed her sense of competitiveness to her family background, "having a sister one year older and my parents and grandparents constantly saying, 'How come your grades are not as good as your sister's?'" she chuckled. But Nooyi did not learn everything early in life. She finds leadership lessons in the unlikeliest of places—including watching her favorite sport of baseball and her beloved team, the New York Yankees.

Nooyi traced her love of baseball to growing up watching cricket. But when she arrived in the United States, there was no bat and ball sport other than baseball. From the first time she saw a game, Nooyi was hooked. "I think it's one of the great sports. I look at so many subtle things when I watch the Yankees. They are the only team I watch in baseball, by the way. I watch how they field, the crispness of the double plays, how they anticipate, how the catcher provides a signal," she explained.

Even in the midst of a discussion about baseball, Nooyi never leaves her true passion behind: leadership. "I watch how [Yankees manager] Joe Girardi or before him Joe Torre can take a bunch of players who all get paid a boatload of money and knit them into a cohesive team so that they don't worry about their individual records but worry about the team. How Joe Torre and now Joe Girardi in such a calm way can manage the team and knit them together toward a common goal. It is a great leadership lesson," she added.

PRIVILEGE AND RESPONSIBILITY

As she leads her team, expands her learning, and elevates the organization, Nooyi has embraced both the privilege and the responsibility of the position she occupies. The privilege is the opportunity to lead a corporation with so many iconic brands. The responsibility comes from the continuous need to grow and improve a colossus with $60 billion in revenues. "At 25 cents or a buck a pop, that's a lot of bags of chips, bottled beverages, and oatmeal bars and containers that we have to sell," Nooyi said. "So the innovation machine has to keep going, keeping people excited."

PepsiCo's products are built around fun, wholesome, and nutritious foods and beverages, "the little pleasures and goodness in life," as Nooyi described them. So in order to attract the best and brightest to the PepsiCo team, the company needs to offer its employees a purpose that goes far beyond the norm. Nooyi has found that incentive for her team through Performance with Purpose and its mission of contributing to the good of society around the globe.

"You can't just say to people, 'Our company provides jobs.' That alone cannot be the motivator. It's got to be more," Nooyi explained. "That's why Performance with Purpose resonates so much, because it is a way for everybody to feel that they can come to PepsiCo and bring their whole selves to work. They don't have to park their selves at the door and be somebody else. They can do their best at work and know they are making a difference to the world. PepsiCo should be a place where you can make a living and have a life. We want everybody to feel that way."

As a leader with purpose Nooyi has guided the company toward embracing a larger vision that goes beyond performance targets. She sees the possibility for PepsiCo to improve people's health, especially fighting both obesity and malnutrition, by broadening the portfolio of products to include healthier options. She also wants the company to help protect the environment and elevate the quality of life for people everywhere.

Nooyi has demonstrated the importance of a CEO embracing and embodying the message, not just in words but also in action. She showed how the unique combination of inspirational and strategic thinking can lead to significant changes in performance and culture.

Most important, Nooyi's communicative and inclusive leadership style demonstrates that although she is the one in the executive office, it is the company, people, mega-brands, and positive effect that can be made everywhere that are important. It is this bigger picture and vision that Nooyi believes truly motivate and inspire— not who sits in the executive chair.

It's not until you discover your potential, your leadership, your capacities—then you can commit to trying to do big things.

—Vicente Fox, former president
of Mexico (2000–2006)

Chapter Four

VICENTE FOX: HUMILITY

A narrow, gravel road led to the sprawling ranch outside of León, Guanajuato, Mexico. There was no gate at the entrance, no visible security detail, only rolling brown landscape that stretched all the way to the horizon. As we approached, our car rumbled across cobblestones that were put in just recently; before that, the driveway had been dirt. The hacienda was large with graceful brick archways and thick stucco walls—not at all ostentatious. It is, first and foremost, a working farm and a family home.

A man in dark slacks and a white open-necked shirt greeted us warmly. His face was touched by the sun, giving him the healthy look of an outdoorsman who grew up close to the land. Even to new friends, he was "Vicente." To the rest of the world, he is former Mexican president Vicente Fox, the first opposition president to break the seventy-one-year iron-fisted rein of the Institutional Revolutionary Party (PRI).

As president of Mexico from 2000 to 2006, Fox ascended to the world stage, associating frequently with leaders such as former president George W. Bush and former British prime minister Tony Blair. He engaged in debates about U.S.-led military action in Iraq and went up against the Bush Administration over assertions that Saddam Hussein had caches of weapons of mass destruction. As a leader in his own party, he pushed for decentralization of the government and instituted checks and balances for the executive branch that previously had held a tight grip on power. He reduced the Mexican government's involvement in areas he felt were better left to the private sector. Under Fox, democracy and openness took root in Mexico.

As a leader, Fox embraced the "heroic aspirations" that he believes are in the soul of every person, not just the powerful and successful. In our conversation he invoked the names of leaders he admires: Mahatma Gandhi, Martin Luther King Jr., Nelson Mandela, and Lech Walesa. "With their humbleness and their sacrifice and their very strong power within themselves, they could not be dictated to by anybody," he commented. "Look at what they accomplished."

Although his own accomplishments are impressive, Fox remains a surprisingly humble man. He never forgot where he came from. With grace, he rose above previous abuses of presidential power in his country and avoided the temptations to become wrapped up in the prestige and privilege of the office. His attitude was inspired by two of his heroes: Ignatius of Loyola, the sixteenth-century Spanish saint who founded the Jesuits and preached compassion and love as the way to win the hearts of others, and his grandfather, a hardworking, driven man who immigrated to Mexico from Ohio and established the ranch where Fox now lives.

By honoring his roots, Fox has maintained the distinction between who he is and what he does—a struggle for many people in positions of authority, including business leaders, for whom the lines between job title and personal identity can easily blur. Even as president of Mexico, Fox remained as accessible as the wide open spaces of his ranch.

For Fox, leaders come in two varieties: from either the camp of Machiavelli, the Italian philosopher and writer who in his work *The Prince* portrayed the political cunning and ruthlessness that can bring respect and authority, or that of Ignatius of Loyola, who believed that leadership is gained through higher ideals. "I can have a conversation with someone and within fifteen minutes tell which group he is in: more on the side of humility or more on the side of severity," Fox said.

Fox put himself on "Loyola's side," believing that the way to win is with "convincing, negotiating, and using strategy." He acknowledged that his leadership style was interpreted by some as weakness. Mexico had been conditioned for seventy-one years by the PRI, which as Mexico's dominant political organization had exercised unfettered power with little or no opposition. When Fox came into the power, he faced criticism from those who were still loyal to the PRI. "They said, 'This is a weak president. He doesn't know how to exercise power. If you get power, you have to exercise it,'" he explained.

In order for Fox to stay true to his beliefs, both philosophical and political, he had to rise above the opposition and criticism as he decentralized the government to share power more broadly. In order to promote a more democratic Mexico, he had to become a certain kind of leader that the country had not seen before. As Fox described his challenges, I was reminded how business leaders in the midst of significant culture change will also face contrarians and cynics who are entrenched in the past and resistant to embracing a new way of thinking and acting. In fact, Fox believes inner strength is one of the most important qualities a leader can possess—more important than education or formal training. "Leadership is having that power within, that inner commitment, and to start moving with it," he said.

WEIGHING THE RISKS

For Fox, voicing his convictions and going public with them were not without risk. Opposing the PRI was not to be taken lightly. In fact, when he first let his political aspirations be known, his father and his brothers cautioned him, warning that the family ranch could be at risk of being seized by the government. "Everybody was afraid in this nation to go against the government," he recalled. The one person in the family who gave him full support was his mother. "She would say, 'Do it, Vicente. Beat the hell out of them. I'm with you all the way.'"

Fox was also urged to step forward by his friend, the late Manuel Clouthier, who had run unsuccessfully for president of Mexico in 1988 and was widely credited for helping to weaken the power of the PRI. "Manuel's core message was it is not enough to create wealth and jobs; the commitment had to be total," Fox explained. "If you want to get rid of the PRI, you have to join in and work and take the risk of doing that. He convinced me."

In March 1988, Fox joined the Partido Acción Nacional (PAN). That same year he ran for and was elected to the federal Chamber of Deputies, representing the Third Federal District in León, Guanajuato. Humility and heroics played equal parts in Fox's political life from the beginning. On the side of humility was a feeling that Fox described as the need to find "where I could do more for others and for the community." He credited his Jesuit education, which taught him that "happiness is when you do things for others. That is where you find happiness and self-satisfaction."

The heroic side manifested in Fox's love of risk taking and his "emotional satisfaction of taking on big challenges that are difficult to accomplish." His voice rose dramatically as he spoke of each person's potential and the possibility of living a life of significance through service to others. "I would think 90 percent of us don't even know how many things we can do and what power we have within us and how far we can go if we are just determined and committed," he commented. "It's not until you discover your potential, your leadership, your capacities—then you can commit to trying to do big things."

As Fox sees it, too many people today live in mediocrity, not knowing they are capable of more. Once they discover their potential for leadership and their innate capabilities, however, they hunger to do more. "You have to start by leading yourself and then really work on yourself so that you are equipped to start moving ahead and doing things. The second step is to have heroic aspirations: big goals to meet, good goals. We've had negative leaders and positive leaders. For example, Hitler had high aspirations, but, of course, negative ones. In the end, those who have negative goals end up failing. Those with good goals, ethical goals, values-based goals, they will get there," Fox commented.

"There are many other leadership qualities. You have to have vision. He who knows where he is heading can do a much better job than he who doesn't know where he is going or what he is going to do. So you have to do this exercise to find out about yourself. Who are you? What are you in this life for? What would you like to do? You need to have that vision of your own life plan. And then you add values like passion and love, which are key ingredients."

THE ROAD TO LEADERSHIP

Leadership, Fox believes, does not belong only to the educated and accomplished or to those who hold positions of authority. All people can be leaders, in their families, at work, and in their communities. "We must start conveying the message that there are many ways to be a leader—not necessarily only the president. It can be in small actions that are very important. When you have all the small actions of leaders, then you can produce great results in building nations," he added. Fox's leadership views coincide with his belief in decentralizing, taking power away from one person—such as the president—and empowering others who have a particular expertise or who are closer to the problem or situation.

Fox learned early in his career about the importance of having a close connection with the people. Soon after he graduated from Universidad Iberoamericana, he took a job with Ford Motor Company, which wanted him to "wear a tie and run an office." After a month, he quit. Much more suited to his personality was a sales job with Coca-Cola, which he took in 1964. Even though his former university classmates were wearing suits and driving Ferraris, Fox was comfortable with his truck and his Coca-Cola uniform. He was among the people, with the shopkeepers and the business owners, where he is most at home even to this day. "In those days, driving the truck, that's the best learning I could have: being with people and being humble," he added.

His humility did not keep him from having big aspirations. From the very beginning, he wanted to run all of Coca-Cola. Although he did not reach that career pinnacle, he did become a marketing executive for Coca-Cola de México in 1969 and then became president of that division in 1974 with responsibility for Latin America. He held that post for five years before deciding to return to the family's ranch and businesses, including vegetable exporting.

Similarly, when he first became active in politics his ultimate goal, although he kept it to himself at the time, was to become president of Mexico one day. For that to happen, Fox and others, including the intellectual and writer Carlos Fuentes, had to work to change the Mexican constitution, which had limited eligibility only to those whose parents were born in Mexico. Although Fox, whose mother had been born in Spain, benefited personally from the constitutional change, he maintained it was not a purely self-serving move. "Nobody said, 'Vicente is working on this to become president.' No, we worked on it because it was the right of every Mexican born here to serve his country and be president."

Looking back, Fox acknowledged the influence of his grandfather for his aspirations, seeing in his example the drive and dedication necessary to reach his goals. A man of few words, his grandfather never learned to speak Spanish, yet he was able to establish a successful ranch. From his grandfather, too, he learned respect for private property. Back when his grandfather was running the ranch, the government took away 90 percent of the family's landholdings. "The government with all legitimacy could come in and take your land and not give you a penny for it," Fox said, shaking his head as if it happened just the other day. Still, his grandfather did not give up or give in. Throughout our conversation, Fox mentioned his grandfather several times. Although his grandfather died when Fox was only seven, the impression the older man made has continued to influence him. "I learned a lot from him, not by speaking to him so much, but seeing him and his attitude and his strength," he explained.

In his hallway, Fox displayed the portraits of two of his other heroes. One was a priest martyr who had stood up to the revolutionaries in Mexico after they closed the churches and banished the priests. In the picture the man stood defiantly, a cigarette in his lips, staring down his accusers. "Such determination to die for his religious beliefs. Such a challenging look. Then one minute later, he's being shot," Fox remarked.

Another is of the actor John Wayne, an icon of countless Western movies. "From my childhood . . . the time you dream about cowboys," he said with a laugh.

It struck me that such a mix of images said a lot about Fox, who in his political career became a bit of a revolutionary himself and, in the process, an icon as well.

THE IMPORTANCE OF HUMILITY

The higher leaders rise, the further they move from where they began. The danger is that success will undermine their humility, leaving them out of touch and disconnected. Fox learned that lesson early in his career, long before he considered public service. The occasion was the ten-year reunion of his university class, an elegant gathering at the University Club on the fashionable Paseo de la Reforma in Mexico City. As the former classmates and their spouses greeted each other, they displayed the outward signs of their wealth and success. "Our wives were in furs and jewels, and everyone had a big Rolex watch and was showing how successful we were," Fox chuckled.

Then a priest who had been a favorite instructor at the university got up to address the group. He opened his remarks by announcing that he was leaving the reunion party. "I love all of you and I love your wives," the priest told them, "but I am totally disappointed in you. You think you are successful but you are not. This is not my teaching. I did not teach you to make money, to have beautiful wives, to have the best clothes, and to come here very presumptuous. That's not what I taught you."

The priest's message rippled through the room like a shock-wave. "Just think about it," the priest continued. "Are you happy with yourself? Are you really following the teaching of the Jesuit education?"

Fox felt the weight of those words strike him as being "absolutely true." Instead of focusing solely on his own success, he decided to devote himself to what he could do for others. To do that effectively, he needed to maintain a connection with the people, to be open and accessible to them, just as he was back when he was driving the Coca-Cola truck.

"There are so many temptations that would undermine your humility. You have to develop that part, work on it all your life. It's easy to fall on the other side, especially when you are in power and have a position. When I was president, I would go into the crowds and talk to people. I still do. I walk down the street. People come up to me. I am very accessible and very easy to reach," Fox said.

As we strolled through León, Fox noticed an elderly woman who looked confused and was probably lost. Without saying a word to his guests, Fox crossed the street, spoke gently to the woman, and guided her in the other direction. She did not seem to recognize him as he bent his tall frame and put his arm around her. To her, he was only a kind gentleman who helped her find her way.

As president, Fox believed it was imperative that he remain close to the people to make sure their needs were met. "We closed the office and went out into the field just to make sure things were happening," he remembered.

Fox's message struck me as being a very important one for business leaders who need to stay connected with people everywhere, from the employees who work for the organization to the customers who buy the products. CEOs who are disconnected from the front line suffer a competitive disadvantage, although they might not realize it at the time. They do not learn firsthand about what is working and what is not. They cannot gather business intelligence from those who are closest to the marketplace. A CEO who sequesters himself away from everyone except the inner circle will be told only what others want him to hear.

Being a leader, Fox said, is not the same as being the one out in front, ahead of the others. He used the example of women in Latin America who, for generations, were the power behind the men. "We have this saying that behind every big man are the women," he explained. "Finally in Latin America we are seeing women by the side of men when they once were always behind."

As he spoke, Fox showed himself to be a student of leadership, a topic he believes must be explored continually. Observing American businesses, he considers it a negative that "too much responsibility and too much power" are typically bestowed on one person, who is then paid millions of dollars a year. "He might have a good idea, but I don't know if that is going in the right direction. Maybe it's better to have a whole team with a lot of ideas and to try to collect them from everyone," he added. "I love the culture in the United States so much. But then I have to accept the power, the force that you develop when each person has such a hunger—such a strong personal initiative to be somebody, to accomplish this, and to go for this goal. That is the engine that moves the United States."

A leader must also know when it is prudent not to exercise power, when the greater good is better served by moderation. Fox gave the example of a project to build a new airport. His administration entered into negotiations with landowners starting at five pesos per square meter, which he called a fair commercial price. When the owners refused to sell their property, the government counteroffered with higher prices until, six months later, it had reached fifty-five pesos.

The advice he received was to expropriate: exercising the government's right to take the land for the common good. But was it the common good, Fox wondered, if only 3 percent of the people in Mexico use air transportation? In the end, he did not expropriate the land and instead opted to build a system of airports within the Mexico City region, which he felt produced a much better return.

"Maybe I was remembering my grandfather who questioned, 'Why should I lose 90 percent of my business?' If you don't have a good purpose, then you cannot sustain your plan," Fox added. "At the very end, you have to go by responsible decisions."

POLL NUMBERS AND CONVICTIONS

Being a leader requires a delicate balance between popularity and one's convictions. In business, if consumers do not like the product and the brand, or if investors do not favor the company, the result could be disaster. In politics, unpopularity undermines a leader's effectiveness and ability to build a coalition, and ultimately will limit the politician's career.

For Fox, poll numbers are nearly an obsession. He studies the numbers the way a sports fan tracks the scoreboard: who's winning and who's losing; who has a comfortable lead. In The Vicente Fox Center of Studies, Library and Museum, as his new presidential library is called, a series of large plasma screens displayed the Gallup numbers for President Barak Obama. At the time, a few weeks after the passage of healthcare reform and in the midst of taking on an overhaul of the financial industry, Obama's popularity was waning.

Fox explained his fascination with polls by recalling his background as a "marketing guy who had to go by the numbers." In politics, he added, "the only measure we have for the customer is the poll. We all try to follow what the customer expects."

He quoted poll statistics off the top of his head, recalling the days after September 11 when former president George W. Bush's approval rating topped 80 percent. In those days, world leaders gathered for summit meetings rose to their feet and applauded when Bush entered the room. "When you have power behind you, you think you can do a lot of things, which is not necessarily true," Fox commented.

Bush, for example, believed Iraq would be an easy battle, which turned out not to be the case. As the war dragged on and then a financial and economic crisis hit, Bush's poll numbers dropped below 30 percent by the end of his term. "All leaders have to battle and struggle to accomplish big goals. If you walk into a battle, you've got to make sure you have a plan—and make sure you are going to win that war," Fox advised.

There are times, however, when a leader's sense of responsibility must outweigh the polls. Then leaders must make decisions that they know are unpopular, and only time will tell whether history vindicates them.

Leaders also face unpopular decisions when they must break from their peers, standing up for their own convictions. Fox encountered this challenge when Mexico was among the Latin American nations on the United Nations Security Council. With the Bush Administration pressing for an invasion of Iraq to oust Saddam Hussein, Mexico and Chile held firm in their opposition. Fox recalled receiving countless phone calls from then-president Bush, then–U.K. prime minister Tony Blair, and others trying to convince him to support the plan for a U.S.-led invasion. Fox said he and Chilean president Ricardo Lagos held firm in their opposition. "I remember well the two key votes [against] were Mexico and Chile," he said. "President Lagos and I would call each other and say, 'Let's not cede to the pressure. Let's stand on our position.' We made each other strong."

CITIZEN FOX

Today, Fox is the first former president in Mexico to keep a public profile. In the past, ex-presidents quietly faded away, sometimes living in exile. Fox broke that tradition by going in the other direction with his presidential library. "We have a misconception of democracy after seventy-one years that says the former president has to be quiet, has to go home, or live outside of Mexico. It's institutional," he said. "That's the practice, that's the culture, and that was what had to be done."

The Vicente Fox Center, which is supported entirely by private donations, focuses primarily on four issues: democracy and freedom, market economies with responsibility, developing public policy in Latin America, and supporting gender equality in the region. The center's holdings include millions of presidential documents and thousands of hours of videos from Fox's time in office. Many scholars in the country have applauded the undertaking, particularly because the practice in the past has not been to keep documents.

Since stepping down from his term in office, Fox has commented on the current president, Felipe Calderon, who, like Fox, is a member of the conservative PAN party. Fox has spoken out in the media to criticize Calderon at times, such as for his failed mission to send the military after drug cartels, and he has applauded his successor for other moves, such as his handling of the H1N1 flu epidemic in early 2010. "My latest effort to expand the concept of democracy in Mexico has to do with accountability," he added. "It has to do with my freedom to speak, to comment, to debate, and to express my public opinion."

In speeches, Fox has acknowledged the shortcomings of his own term as president. Mexico did not enjoy the double-digit growth of other emerging nations, although he did accomplish economic stability and reduced poverty by building a modest middle class. "In the case of Latin America, stability brings you strength in the currency so people's assets don't lose value. Stability is where we human beings perform better. You need stability, you need certainty so that every person performs at his best," he observed.

In the same breath, he acknowledged that every leader's term is influenced by circumstances that may very well be beyond any individual's control. "I was lucky to be part of the last ten years when the world performed better than any other time in history," he said. "How many people have done great things and they don't show anything for their results? And others had the favorable winds behind them and they got all the credit."

Vicente Fox leaned back in his chair and surveyed the landscape just beyond the courtyard where he was relaxing with guests. Overhead a plane droned and hammers from a renovation project at the ranch pounded a staccato beat. With his heroic aspirations, Fox tried to accomplish as much as he could. His legacy, however, may be less about what he did and more about who he was: the first opposition president elected in what was hailed as the country's most honest and fair election.

"You end up understanding that six years is nothing in the span of life of the nation. You're just part of the effort of one or two generations," he said stoically. "There are no miracles or shortcuts in development."

As a leader, Fox put his ideas into action in an effort to be a positive influence for change and greater openness in his country. Then, like all leaders, he had to face the reality that another would come after him and take the reins. In government or in business, the best that leaders can do is to act as guardians and trustees for the time that they are given.

You have to care for people—for the organization as a whole and for the individual. When the soldiers know you care for them, and they know you are competent, they will literally put their lives on the line for you.
—Lieutenant General Franklin L. "Buster" Hagenbeck, retired superintendent, West Point

Chapter Five

LIEUTENANT GENERAL FRANKLIN L. "BUSTER" HAGENBECK: COMPASSION

Visiting the United States Military Academy, even for just an afternoon, you feel its storied past that dates back to General George Washington. A long military tradition means discipline—physical, mental, and moral—and expectations of excellence for each of the one thousand or so cadets who graduate each year as second lieutenants serving in the United States Army. The legacy of the institution is leadership, which is what brought me here to interview the superintendent in charge: Lieutenant General Franklin L. "Buster" Hagenbeck, a man with nearly four decades of military experience, including as a general commanding troops on the ground in Afghanistan.

Facing the lush green parade grounds are statues of generals who were once cadets here: Dwight Eisenhower, George Patton, and Douglas MacArthur. For these men, leadership meant command and control, a style that is today considered a relic in the business world but presumed to be alive and well in the military. Before I met General Hagenbeck in early summer 2010, four months before he retired as superintendent of West Point, I had expected that he, too, would fit the command-and-control mode. Yet from the moment we met, he dispelled military stereotypes, introducing himself by his nickname, "Buster," and dispensing with the formalities he richly deserves by virtue of his rank and accomplishments.

Fit and trim at the age of sixty from being a lifelong athlete, Hagenbeck had an easy accessibility about him no matter what the topic, from sports to his long military career. In conversation he was more interested in learning about others than doing all the talking.

What was most striking about Hagenbeck, as we discussed the cadets, the academy, and the U.S. Army, was his compassion. This general may have worn three stars on his epaulets but he had his heart on his sleeve. Hagenbeck has had soldiers die under his command, sometimes right in front of him. In the moment he had to deal with not only the loss of that life, but also the emotional toll on those under his command who have lost a comrade. "When the fight is going on, you get through it. Afterward you grieve," Hagenbeck told me, his eyes moistening but his voice calm and his gaze steady.

Hagenbeck faced the fight of his life in the rugged mountainous terrain on the border between Afghanistan and Pakistan in late February 2002. As the commanding general of the 10th Mountain Division, Hagenbeck led the mission known as Operation Anaconda, his last major ground battle before returning stateside as a three-star general. As Hagenbeck told the story of intense battle, he spoke of the importance of strategy and training to ensure that people on the ground can carry out the mission and do what is expected of them.

Simply put, conditions were brutal. The snow piled up at night, and windchills dropped the temperature to minus 20 degrees Fahrenheit, although during the day it could warm up to as much as 60 degrees. American Special Forces and conventional troops from the 101st Airborne and the 10th Mountain Divisions, along with allied forces, waited throughout a long night to launch a predawn strike. They targeted three villages in the Shahi-Kot Valley, where intelligence reports had identified between 150 and 250 foreign al-Qaida. The mission was to rout them out and cut off their escape routes across the mountains. Maps of the area that were drawn by the British years before showed the border between Afghanistan and Pakistan. To the local tribesmen, such maps and boundaries were meaningless; this was their land. Likewise, foreign al-Qaida criss-crossed the terrain of steep mountains and deep valleys pitted with caves, going from one country to the other and back again.

At a remote airfield, with the Hindu Kush mountains as a backdrop, Hagenbeck waited with his troops to begin the fight that was expected to last three, maybe five days. Throughout a long sleepless night of watching and waiting, he mentally reviewed the strategy to launch the raid at four o'clock the next morning. The helicopter crews, with the exception of two groups that were veterans of the Gulf War, were considered too inexperienced to fly against anti-aircraft fire during the daylight hours. At dawn or dusk they could gain an advantage against the enemy that was already advancing into the high ground, its numbers swelling well beyond the initial intelligence report estimates.

At midnight, just a few hours before the attack was to begin, Hagenbeck received a call from Special Ops reporting that foreign al-Qaida were now estimated at four hundred and possibly more. Special Forces asked the general to launch immediately; a quick strike could take the enemy out. "If you go in there, you'll tip our hand," Hagenbeck warned. Keeping a secret was impossible in Afghanistan, especially with nine allied nations converging in one place. The al-Qaida knew they were coming; the only elements of surprise were time and direction.

Just before dawn, the first of the helicopters went in along with CH-47 Chinooks transporting troops. Immediately they drew heavy fire. Despite the barrage, the forces were able to secure most of the landing zones within the first two hours except for those in the southern region of the target area. Within the first thirty minutes of fighting in the southern section, twenty-eight soldiers were wounded.

Grounded at the airbase because the second airlift was delayed by heavy fighting, Hagenbeck had to rely on his commanders as his eyes and ears. Limited surveillance information from unmanned Predator drones provided enough intelligence for the general to receive real-time advice from Washington, ranging from reinforcing the lines during the daytime to withdrawing immediately—and everything in between. Hagenbeck needed to speak with his commanders on the ground. Lieutenant Colonel Paul LaCamera, the newest battalion commander out of the 10th Mountain Division, told him not to send in Medivac helicopters for the wounded; it was still too dangerous. "We can save these guys," LaCamera assured him.

Hagenbeck thought back to when troops from the 10th Mountain Division had trained with the cadets at West Point during summer 2001 and medics had worked with trauma units in New York City. That training made the difference in Hagenbeck's mind. It wasn't just a hope and wish; these men could be saved because LaCamera's battalion had acquired the skills to accomplish the task.

Hagenbeck put his faith in the troops on the ground, letting them fight the battle their way, while he and his leaders planned to get the wounded out. His consolation was a phrase that's often used in the army: "Mission first, people always." He knew his commanders would accomplish the mission without taking unnecessary risks with their subordinates. At dusk, the twenty-eight wounded were successfully evacuated despite rocket-propelled grenades being shot at the helicopters from one hundred feet away.

After seventy-two hours with virtually no sleep, Hagenbeck made his way to a cot in a converted Soviet hangar that had no electricity or running water. After thirty minutes of rest, he was awakened. The look on the soldier's face told him the news was bad. Helicopters had come under heavy fire on landing, causing the pilots to pull away quickly. After a headcount, it was discovered a man was missing, apparently having fallen undetected from the helicopter ramp. The missing man was Navy SEAL Neil Roberts.

Intelligence indicated Roberts had been captured and killed but not without putting up a valiant fight, as Hagenbeck would later learn. Despite the danger, Special Ops was going in with Army Ranger support to retrieve Roberts's body. One of the army's unwavering principles is "leave no man behind." The first Ranger off the helicopter was shot and killed. The others battled the enemy in snow that ranged in depth from two feet to drifts of up to eight to ten feet. Finally, they were able to recover Roberts's body.

As the battle raged, American and allied forces were outnumbered by several hundred, perhaps as many as one thousand, al-Qaida. Instead of the two or three dozen caves that Hagenbeck had been told to expect, there were as many as 130 of them, large and small, riddling the mountain sides.

For fourteen days, American and allied troops engaged in brutally intense combat. Finally, on the fifteenth day, after sixty casualties, including eight killed, the area was secured. Foreign al-Qaida not killed or captured quickly dispersed. In the caves, troops found huge caches of weapons and computer files yielding intelligence.

COMPETENCY AND CARING

Operation Anaconda was a success in terms of mission accomplished, securing a strategically important position on the Afghanistan-Pakistan border and preventing a buildup of foreign al-Qaida in the area. Well-trained and prepared soldiers executed the battle plan under brutal conditions while facing far greater numbers of the enemy than originally estimated. Yet listening to Hagenbeck tell this story of his last major campaign on the battlefield, what was most striking was his genuine concern for his troops and the emotion with which he spoke about the soldiers lost in battle.

The two qualities Hagenbeck sees as most essential to lead effectively are competency and caring. He attributed his own understanding of both to a mentor who made a powerful impact throughout his career: General Hugh Shelton, a former chairman of the Joint Chiefs of Staff, with whom he served five times. "He was the first one to impart competency and caring," Hagenbeck explained with admiration in his voice.

Competency is the foundation of every successful leader in any field. "You have to work harder than anybody else, and you have to be smarter than anybody else," Hagenbeck said. "You have to pull out all the stops to continuously learn; it doesn't end. You really have to know what you are doing, and people have to understand—and they will."

Hagenbeck's competency was well proven over the years, with Hagenbeck serving in the 25th Infantry Division, the 101st and 82nd Airborne Divisions, the 10th Mountain Division, and the U.S. Army Training and Doctrine Command. Throughout nearly four decades of military service, Hagenbeck held commands at every level, from company through division—and, in the process, moved his family twenty-six times (the mother of all job transfers). Hagenbeck said yes to going wherever the military needed him.

As a soldier he was in his share of battles, and he knows what it's like to be shot at and have bombs go off around him. Yet competency alone, no matter how impressive, will not win the hearts and minds of comrades and subordinates. To do that requires a second leadership attribute: caring.

"You have to care for the people—for the organization as a whole and for the individual," Hagenbeck explained. "When the soldiers know you care for them, and they know you are competent, they will literally put their lives on the line for you." One of the greatest risks for any leader is to charge up a mountain only to discover that no one is following. Potential followers are much more motivated if they know the leader cares for them.

Having others put their faith and trust in a leader is both a blessing and a burden. The commanding officer relies on subordinates to carry out the mission, even when that means putting them in harm's way. "You will always second-guess yourself, or leaders will, if you could have done something differently to have saved a life," Hagenbeck said. "You have to be extraordinarily prepared and competent before you go into battle. You have to make split-moment decisions."

With preparedness comes the inner peace of knowing that everything humanly possible has been done to keep people safe, to save as many lives as possible. At the same time, death is an outcome of war. "You go in there with your eyes wide open. You hope it never happens, but it does," Hagenbeck added.

A Soldier by Choice

Like the cadets at West Point today, Hagenbeck enrolled in the academy during a time of war. For him, it was the summer of 1967, and the Vietnam conflict was raging. As a senior at the academy, Hagenbeck selected the infantry as his desired branch in which to serve and chose a unit that was in Vietnam. By the time he finished training, however, the army was "standing down," that is, beginning its pullout from Vietnam. Instead, Hagenbeck and his wife, Judy—his childhood sweetheart whom he married right after graduation—went to Hawaii with the 25th Infantry Division. After two years, Hagenbeck was a first lieutenant and a "hotshot platoon leader." When Shelton, who was a brand new major and brigade operations officer, asked him to become his assistant, Hagenbeck wasn't sure it was the right move. "I said, 'Sir, I can't do that; it will hurt my career.' He said, 'Buster, you don't have a career. Be here on Monday,'" Hagenbeck remembered with a laugh.

While serving in the military, Hagenbeck enrolled in Florida State to get his master's degree and served as an assistant football coach to the legendary Bobby Bowden of the Florida State Seminoles. "There is a structure to Bowden, a discipline, a way to get things done," Hagenbeck explained. "He delegates, but if he needs to get involved in something, all the way to telling a quarterback what his footwork ought to be like, he will do it." Reflecting on what he learned from Bowden, Hagenbeck spoke of the necessary balance between allowing people to figure things out for themselves and stepping in to clarify when necessary.

At the academy, Hagenbeck's passion and ability in athletics set an example for cadets who are expected to play a sport, stressing the importance of competition, physical strength, agility, as well as something Hagenbeck called the "warrior ethos," which he described as "never accept defeat, never quit, and never leave a fallen comrade."

When he became superintendent of the academy in 2006, however, he found some cadets were happy just to play a sport but were not concerned about winning. He saw this as an "indictment of society," in which kids are given trophies "just for showing up." The warrior ethos focuses on winning, with lessons that translate directly from playing field to battlefield—and to the corporate world.

"I've been in a lot of fights. Never on the night before a battle did I sit up with my sergeants and captains and say, 'Gee, I hope we win tomorrow.' Losing is just not an option," Hagenbeck said. "I think the athletic field helps to instill that, winning the right way."

At West Point, the importance of competition and conditioning has changed the components of class ranking over the years. When Hagenbeck was a cadet in the 1960s, 90 percent of ranking was based on academics, with the remaining 10 percent split between physical condition and military training. Today, academics accounts for 60 percent, with physical and military making up 40 percent. Still, West Point has not diluted its academic standards, Hagenbeck said, pointing to a *Forbes* article in 2010 that rated the academy as the top college in the United States, beating out the Ivy Leagues. "We are proud of our academics. We have two Rhodes Scholars again this year; we are fourth in the nation in the production of Rhodes Scholars," he observed. "We are always going to have bright kids, but it is so much more than that."

An important part of a cadet's preparation is self-analysis to explore what it means to be a leader. To Hagenbeck, that means being authentic and genuine, knowing your strengths and weaknesses, and understanding how other people perceive you. "It starts with being strategic in nature, and you have to be visionary. You have to be able, in our terms, to give mission statements and commander's intent. You have to be able to empower the people below you. The bedrock foundation of it all is honesty and integrity.

These cadets, with very few exceptions, walk away with an understanding of that," he added.

Being a Leader

West Point creates leaders who will face life-or-death choices in the field. As superintendent of the academy, Hagenbeck provided perspective on the age-old question: are leaders born or are they made? Hagenbeck cited the army's behavioral scientists whose studies indicate about 30 percent of a leader's ability is inherited and the other 70 percent is learned.

Development encompasses what is taught, including through unique experiences for cadets, such as being put in charge of classmates and subordinates. Upperclassmen are sent to the army for three to four weeks of on-the-job training during the summer or go overseas for cultural immersion in more than fifty countries, doing primarily humanitarian work. Development happens through experience-based learning. Although the classroom can lay the foundation, real training occurs on the job, which is equally true in the corporate world.

After graduation, development continues for the newly minted second lieutenants, who train for about six months with one of the army's sixteen branches, such as aviation, infantry, armored, or signal corps. During this period they are exposed to sergeants who share their knowledge and experiences to help the new officers get ready for their commands. "They [new officers] understand they are going to have opportunities as a new graduate that no other college graduates are having. They are going to be in charge of thirty to forty soldiers, life and limb," Hagenbeck remarked. "We teach them that as a commander, you are responsible for all your unit does or fails to do. That goes all the way to the top, just as I am responsible for all that happens here."

Without honesty and integrity, Hagenbeck added, a leader cannot gain the trust and respect of subordinates who are ultimately responsible for accomplishing the mission. Honesty and integrity are embedded in the West Point culture through a strict honor code, which states that a cadet does not lie, cheat, or steal, or tolerate those who do. "We know that everyone comes from different backgrounds; we view that as developmental," Hagenbeck said. "Cadets know the honor code. They are the ones who determine the guilt or innocence of their classmates and then make recommendations on whether the cadet should be separated completely from the academy or whether there should be discretion taken," such as probation and the removal of privileges.

Accountability and responsibility are not only for one's own actions, but also for those of one's comrades. A cadet who knows about a cheating incident, for example, but remains quiet about it is considered just as guilty. As commanders in the field one day, they ultimately will be responsible for the actions of the soldiers under their command. For Hagenbeck, if something had happened on his watch, he stood ready to take the fall. How many corporate leaders, I wondered, would say the same thing of themselves?

Asked to comment on episodes in the business world, such as the fraud that brought down Enron and the greed on Wall Street that may have contributed to the financial crisis through the creation of high-risk investment instruments, Hagenbeck was neither self-righteous nor judgmental. "It's disconcerting but not surprising," he observed. "To a large degree, I think that's human nature. The way you have to overcome it is to create a culture where it is not tolerated. From our perspective here at West Point, we have much more control and are able to do that."

Hagenbeck is also a big believer in directly connecting with all levels that serve under him, a parallel I could easily draw to senior executives at companies today. "A typical leadership charge is communication, from giving speeches to eating lunch in the mess hall with cadets to find out what's going on," he explained.

Creating alignment starts with the top with senior leadership. Leaders must communicate the mission and purpose—what

Hagenbeck called the "commander's intent"—while also providing guidance to those who will carry it out. "We will typically give bright lines—right and left limits of what they can do. We tell them, 'Be creative and go out and get it done and report back,'" he added.

Essential in any organization are people who will speak the truth and not just what they think the boss wants to hear. Corporate CEOs often find it frustrating that people are reluctant to give honest feedback, especially when the information is difficult or unpleasant. If a leader asks, "How are things going?" no one wants to be the bearer of bad news.

Hagenbeck brought the point home in a humorous way. "I've been a general for a long time, since 1997. I go to great lengths to hire people who will tell me the truth. It starts with my military assistant or my aide, if you will, and I've been saying this for years. I tell them, 'If I am walking down the hall of the Pentagon and somebody tells me my fly is down, I'm firing you. You've been with me all day long, and you didn't have the gumption to tell me.' That's a silly little story, but you have to have people who will tell you what you need to know."

Although certain people may be relied on to provide intelligence about what is happening in the field, that does not preclude or excuse the leader from doing his or her own fact-finding. "Spend a lot of time away from your desk. Go out and see; talk to everyone from the bottom up," Hagenbeck advised. "You have to be smart enough to know how to make those kinds of checks to see if they need help. Things can get misunderstood down the line. You make yourself available."

Like every leader, Hagenbeck has made his share of mistakes. As is the case with many leaders, his stemmed from giving a second chance to someone instead of letting him or her go immediately. "I've been guilty of this two or three different times. I hate to use the word 'firing,' but not getting rid of people as quickly as I should have—cut my losses. Sometimes I go the extra mile and give the extra chance when, intuitively and based on my experience, I know they are not going to be able to do it," he explained. "That does not help the organization." A leader must always focus on the whole, the entire organization, advancing its mission rather than just the individual parts.

A Lasting Legacy

When we spoke, Hagenbeck's time at West Point and with the military was coming to an end. Looking around his office, which was ringed by large portraits of previous West Point superintendents, I was struck by the realization that although the general was at the academy for a distinct period of time, he was really part of a continuum of excellence and leadership. A few months after our meeting, Hagenbeck's picture would go up on the wall, joining such historic figures as General MacArthur and Robert E. Lee, who graduated first in his class at West Point and returned to serve as superintendent until 1855.

For every soldier, there comes a point when it is time to take off the uniform. For Hagenbeck that day came on July 19, 2010. With so much personal history tied up in his career, it might have seemed difficult for Hagenbeck to leave. Yet he was ready. "I feel pretty good about what I've done. This is a real conscious decision," he said, then added, laughing, "It's important to pick your time—go out on top."

Just as Hagenbeck's impact will linger beyond his time as superintendent, the same can be said for certain cadets who, through their lives and service, have made a lasting impression. Hagenbeck told the emotional story of the funeral at the academy held for Second Lieutenant Emily Perez, a platoon leader and the first female graduate of West Point to die in Iraq. Hearing the academy's historic school song performed at Perez's funeral, Hagenbeck cringed at the line, "Guide us, thy sons, aright."

"This was exactly thirty years after female cadets had started to come here in 1976, and yet our [school song] had not changed," he recalled. Although he met with some resistance from those who did not want to tamper with tradition, Hagenbeck successfully campaigned for the lyrics to be changed to "Guide us, thine own, aright," to make the song gender neutral and reflective of today's army.

During his time, Hagenbeck has been present at many such funerals for cadets. At the time of our conversation, he was preparing for a ceremony for yet another cadet who had died in Iraq just a few days before our meeting. As the superintendent, Hagenbeck was there to console the family and also to honor the choice that this young officer made. "I know what these kids want to do," he said. "To a person, they want to do what they are doing."

As a young cadet himself many years ago, Hagenbeck knew firsthand the call to serve and the sacrifice that may entail. Even after four decades in the army, from his first post in Hawaii to commanding a ground operation in the middle of a cold Afghan winter, Hagenbeck would do it all over again. For him, there is no greater reward than knowing he has done his best and made a difference. "Doing something bigger than yourself, doing something for the nation, having a singular purpose—I don't think anything could beat that," he reflected. "That's why I've been at it for so long."

Leaving through the gates of West Point on the day of my visit, I thought back on Lieutenant General Hagenbeck and his two distinct but complementary qualities of leadership: competency and caring. His competency was unquestionable, from nearly forty years in the military, including intense battlefield experience. Caring stemmed from commitment to every member of his team, ensuring that each person was trained and ready for the mission ahead—and always remembering that people come before the mission. As a leader, Hagenbeck showed what it means to have the grace and self-awareness to rise above himself to represent something much larger, both an organization and an ideal: to subjugate himself to the greater good.

The most important thing to me was to teach self-discipline. Guys have got to be disciplined on the field and off the field. . . . I don't coach football; I coach kids.

—Coach John McKissick, Summerville
High School, Summerville, South Carolina; the
"winningest" coach in football

Chapter Six

COACH JOHN MCKISSICK: BUILDING TEAMS

A high school athletic department may not be the first place you'd think of when studying characteristics of the world's best leaders. Yet anyone who has ever played sports at any level, from Little League to college athletics, can tell you there are lessons imparted on the playing field that apply to any competitive arena, including business.

The journey to find the "winningest" coach in football led to Summerville, South Carolina, population forty-five thousand, where for nearly sixty years John McKissick has coached the Summerville "Green Wave." With a cumulative total of 576 victories (as of the end of the 2009 season), McKissick stands out. No other coach at the high school, college, or professional level—not even legends such as Vince Lombardi, Paul "Bear" Bryant, Joe Paterno, or Bobby Bowden—can even come close.

What is it about McKissick and his Green Wave? What is his secret to producing football prodigies? Granted, at the age of eighty-three at the time of our conversation, McKissick had been at it for a while. When he started at Summerville in 1952, Harry Truman was president and Studebakers were still being made. But a lifetime of experience is not the sole reason for his success. Rather, like any great leader, McKissick is an extraordinary team-builder and developer of people. Throughout his coaching career he has been driven by an abiding sense of purpose and a deep desire to help his young players reach their fullest potential.

At one point in our interview, McKissick stepped out of his office for a moment and into the hallway of the high school where students were passing classes. "Hey, Coach!" a young man called out. "Next year, I'm playing for you!" The student turned and walked backward a few steps as he continued down the hall. "I'm ready, and I'm playing for you."

Reflecting on those words, I couldn't help but wonder: what business leader wouldn't want to hear the same thing from his team?

As a team builder, McKissick has exhibited an uncanny ability to mold, motivate, and lead others. His first priority is to engage his team. "I don't coach football," McKissick said, "I coach kids." He knows that one of the biggest motivations for any individual is a sense of belonging to something bigger than one's self. For the players on Summerville's Green Wave that means being part of a winning legacy.

McKissick does not just preach work ethic and discipline, he embodies it, just as he did as a young coach a half-century ago when he would square off against his players on the line. Tanned and fit, McKissick still works closely with the players and also shows the ropes to his assistant coaches. Among the lessons he has passed on to his assistants is how to strike the right balance between discipline and encouragement. As a team-builder it is truly about other people and not about him. At the same time, McKissick brings the fullness of his life experiences to his role as coach and mentor.

LEARNING FROM ADVERSITY

Tough people come from tough situations, McKissick believes. Growing up in a small town in South Carolina during the Great Depression, the second of three sons of hardworking parents, he learned early on what it meant to lose everything. It was around Christmas 1929, a couple of months after the stock market crashed. Hard times had caused his father's soda bottling business to fail. And as if that wasn't bad enough, the family arrived home in the early evening to find only the smoldering remains of their house. Nothing was left to salvage.

"You learn from adversity. I don't care what profession you're in, you're going to have some adversity," McKissick observed. "When things go wrong, I say, 'Learn from it.' If handled correctly, this can be a great teaching tool. If not, then it will threaten your will to go on."

Rather than becoming embittered or discouraged, McKissick overcame the hardships of his youth and found a way to better his life. From his parents, he learned the value of hard work. From the army, which drafted him at age eighteen in 1943, he learned physical discipline. And from the game of football, he learned to be a leader, first as a player and later as a coach.

Although coaching is clearly his calling, McKissick first started out in a different direction. After the army, he attended Presbyterian College in Clinton, South Carolina, on scholarship, and played football and baseball and also wrestled. Graduating with a bachelor's degree in economics, McKissick took a job with a finance company as an adjuster. "I didn't know what an adjuster was coming out of college. I found out it was a collector," he recalled. Remembering the hard times that his family endured during the Depression, McKissick knew he was not cut out for this job. "I felt empathy for people who couldn't pay their bills. I didn't want to repossess their cars and refrigerators."

His love of athletics led McKissick to Summerville. He applied for the high school coaching job in May 1952, got married to his fiancée Joan Carter in June, and accepted the position in Summerville in July. "After I got the job, I asked [the superintendent], 'Why did y'all hire me with all the other people who had experience who wanted the job?' He told me, 'You didn't ask how much it paid.'"

In order to prove himself and keep the job, McKissick knew what he had to do: win. He started out strong with hard work and a burning passion to succeed. He vowed never to let the other coaches outwork or outprepare him. The discipline he demanded of himself carried over into his expectations for his team—not to win, necessarily, but to be prepared and willing to give their all.

"The most important thing to me was to teach self-discipline. Guys have got to be disciplined on the field and off the field. I think that's the biggest thing, being mentally and physically disciplined," McKissick observed. "I was a paratrooper in the army. Going through jump school, that was a lot of discipline. I think I brought that to coaching. They could see when I first started, and even now, that being a paratrooper, I was in shape physically. When I was younger, I could square off down the line with them. I think that impresses a young person."

From the beginning, McKissick distinguished himself as a hands-on leader. As the new coach at Summerville, he made it a point to meet every student at the school who might be interested in playing football and joining the team. As the Green Wave racked up victories, recruiting new players was never a problem. The desire to play for a winning team may be the prime and most obvious motivator for signing up, but there are deeper forces at work here.

One of the most effective ways to create an engaged workforce is through a common purpose. Individuals—whether employees or football players—who embrace the mission of the group move beyond their own self-interests to focus on the good of the team or organization.

All good leaders are lifelong learners, and McKissick has always been a devoted student of the game. In the early days, he modeled his plays after those of Bud Wilkinson, coach of the Oklahoma Sooners, whom he viewed as a role model. As he coached the Green Wave, McKissick adopted the same split-T offense that Wilkinson used.

When it came to inspiring his players, McKissick thought of Vince Lombardi, "who was good with words, and his words meant something every time he spoke." Thinking back to his own high school days, he remembered how his coach "always looked like he was having fun. You've got to make it fun," McKissick added.

Even today, McKissick keeps learning by viewing films of previous games and revising the playbook to suit the different lineup of players each year. He listens to his young assistant coaches for new ideas and readily shares with them the wisdom he has gained. Most of all, he never tires of engaging the players. "You work with kids, they'll keep you young," he said.

Building a Team

As team-builder, coach, and mentor, McKissick's success plays out in the numbers—and not just the wins versus losses. Because so many students want to play for him, his football squad can be as large as ninety or even one hundred players, which is considered huge for a high school team.

"When I first started coaching, kids used to come out for football to get out of work. They were dairy farmers around here; it was a farming community. Now, if they come out for football it is work. I think the hardest way to get a college education is on a football scholarship," he commented.

As a leader, McKissick attracts and inspires students who want to play for him and are willing to go through the drills and discipline to earn a place on his bench. "I have rules and regulations that they have to go by, and if they go by them they are going to get a uniform whether they are good players or not," he explained. Showing up is not enough. Team members must demonstrate a willingness to learn, to try, and to adhere to a code that McKissick expects of every player without exception.

McKissick described his code as "to live clean, think clean, and stop doing all the things that will destroy them physically, mentally, and morally, and to start doing things that will make them cleaner, finer, and more competent." The coach rattled off the words quickly as if he had said them a million times to thousands of boys. He followed with an argument that he has made countless times: "That's not a sacrifice. I tell them that all the time. 'I'm helping you be a better person and a better player.' "

Love of the game creates a learning environment in which no one gives up on the player who doesn't "get it." Practice and repetition build skills and competency. Teammates mentor each other as second- and third-stringers learn from and mimic the star players. Although talent and accomplishment determine who is on the field and who is on the bench, the rising tide of victory raises the ability and intensity of everyone on the team.

"The guys with character and the passion and all, they set an example for the other guys," McKissick remarked. "If you can get one like that it's catching. If you get a great receiver and he's making all kinds of acrobatic catches, then the other ones are going to be trying, too."

During a game when the score widens to a comfortable lead, McKissick will turn to his second- and third-string players to take the field, partly as a reward for progress made and to give them a chance to show what they can do. Who plays in a particular game, however, is ultimately decided by the challenge faced in the moment. The toughest competition requires the most experienced and capable players. It's a life lesson that McKissick preaches to his team. He always reminds the players that there is no room in football for a "me attitude." Although he recognizes and rewards individual efforts, he is also adamant that every player must put the good of the group ahead of his own self-interest.

In all his years of coaching, McKissick has never cut a player from his team. The only ones who leave are those who drop out. Anyone who comes to practice and lives up to expectations will keep his spot on the team and get a chance to show what he can do.

Over the years, some members of the Green Wave have gone on to the pros, and many more have played on the college level. Yet, contrary to most thinking, McKissick said he doesn't treat those who show particular promise any differently than the other players. There can be no favoritism when it comes to players with potential because a sense of equality is what builds team spirit. "A fourteen-, fifteen-, or sixteen-year-old kid will look up to you if you're fair with them and treat them all alike. On the surface, they're different. But if you treat everybody the same, you won't have a problem," he explained.

Playing for McKissick and the victorious Green Wave doesn't guarantee a spot on a college football team. For many players, their careers will end in high school. "I tell them all the time, I believe in setting goals, and I believe in putting them a little out of reach, but never out of sight. If you're playing for Summerville High School, that doesn't mean you are going to get a college scholarship. If it happens, if you are good enough, that will be a bonus," he said.

Throughout his coaching career, McKissick has modeled a winning attitude that he believes will shape his players for success in life beyond football. "They are better prepared because of the discipline, the self-esteem, and the pride of having been a part of something that's successful," he added. "I could name a hundred really successful people who came through this program, and they weren't all first-stringers." Being part of the team, however, was an unforgettable experience, yielding life lessons that fostered future success.

McKissick's leadership playbook also stresses the importance of building a coalition among various stakeholders in order to win their support. In his case, that has meant engaging the school board, superintendent, principals, and parents. With their backing, Summerville High has developed a strong football program, which draws fans from across the community. "In Summerville on a Friday night, you've got the whole community there. I think that makes a difference," he said. "The kids enjoy the big crowds. Then the players go to church on Sunday or uptown to the drugstore and people pat them on the back. They like that. It gives a young person a sense of pride."

With the players surrounded by support and encouragement, an environment is created in which they want to try even harder to succeed and to win. A winning team attracts more support, which allows the team to thrive—creating a virtuous cycle.

TALLYING WINS, DEALING WITH LOSSES

From the very first game in 1952, McKissick and his Green Wave met with success, winning 27–0. They ended the season with ten wins, no losses, and one tie. More winning seasons followed in 1953, 1954, and 1955 when Summerville won its first state championship, which McKissick considered "the greatest thing" at the time. Then came the realization: now that they'd reached the top, the tough part would be staying there. "When I got there, I felt I had to do it every year," he added.

Every time the Green Wave team competes, however, there is always the possibility of losing. Not even the "winningest" coach has victories all the time. McKissick had his first losing season in 1957. The record for that year was an abysmal 1–8–1. Then he faced the tough battle to rebuild the confidence of the team and the support of the community. He prepared hard, reviewing films of the 1957 games, focusing on those who would be returning. Never had he been so eager for the season to start, to give his players a chance to redeem themselves. Motivating a demoralized team that has already tasted victory requires more than just a pep talk and some off-the-cuff inspiration. The team will turn to the coach who must think, act, and live as if victory not only is possible but is ensured.

"I think it's important for kids to be successful. That's why they keep score, I guess. But you can't stress all the time, 'We've got to beat the other team.' I never say something like that. I say, 'You get out there and play as hard as you can play.' I'm not going to ask for 110 percent or 100 percent, but play as hard as you can and we'll probably be successful. If you don't play as hard as you can play, then we might not be successful. I don't say you've got to win. I would never say that," McKissick commented.

Winning carries its own rewards, and losing has its consequences, such as a tough practice on Saturday morning to make up for Friday night's mistakes. Not only is losing inevitable at times, but also it is necessary in order to learn life lessons and to improve as a player. "When we have failure and adversity, if they have worked hard and put a lot into it, it hurts them. You don't want it to hurt them, but you see them crying. If you put a lot into it, you feel bad about losing. As my daddy used to say, 'Son, if you don't put something in the bucket, how are you going to get anything out of it?'" McKissick added.

"You might have one or two out of ninety who wouldn't take it real hard because they slid through practice. They took it easy. But the majority who worked hard—and even the ones who didn't play, but who worked hard in practice—they take it pretty hard."

When it comes to laying blame for a loss, McKissick holds himself fully accountable. "I say coaches lose games; players don't lose games. I never say, 'If they had caught that pass we would have won.' It should never come down to that. I think coaches lose. If everything is equal, the best-coached team will win."

When the game is on, it's up to the players to execute. Sometimes they are victorious, such as during McKissick's first five years when the Green Wave won fifty-two games and lost only two. And sometimes the result is defeat. After a victorious 11–2 season in 2009, Summerville lost the state championship game even though the team was ahead by twenty-one points at the end of the first half. "Things happen. You teach them not to fumble, but they are going to fumble," McKissick said, shaking his head.

Lessons from the Coach

At the time of our conversation, Coach McKissick was looking ahead to spring practice and then starting up again in the fall. As he contemplated the upcoming season, it was clear that retirement was the last thing on McKissick's mind. More than anything, his attitude revealed the secrets behind his lifelong success: single-minded determination, a competitive nature, love of the game, and sights always set on more wins than losses. These attributes are applicable to any playing field, from the gridiron to the corporate arena.

Looking over the span of McKissick's long and successful career, it was also clear that the hard times that he experienced in his young life kept him grounded. He maintained the distinction between what he wanted and what he needed. As a result, McKissick never chased after a pot of gold someplace else when he had his own green pasture right where he was. Even when McKissick received offers from larger schools, including the elite military college The Citadel, as well as Presbyterian College, his alma mater, he turned them all down to stay at Summerville, where he and his wife raised their two daughters.

McKissick found success his own way: an unparalleled record for any coach in the game and nearly sixty years in a sport he loves more than any other. If success is found in true satisfaction and making a meaningful difference in the lives of others, McKissick sets the standard.

On his right hand, McKissick wears a large ring with the number 500 set in diamonds against a green background. It was a gift from a former player in honor of his five-hundredth victory, which put him in the record books and set off a flurry of national media attention. "Every time we go uptown, he keeps telling me, 'I want to give you one that says 600,'" McKissick said with a grin. "All I want is one that says 577—just one more game."

Pursuing one victory at a time is how McKissick has gotten to where he is with consistency, discipline, and a strong work ethic.

"I've always tried to do it one at a time," he added. "It's a hard job to keep the kids from thinking down the line. Same in life or anything else: you've got to take care of what is happening now."

His qualities as a leader make McKissick's story bigger than just football. There are lessons here for leaders who want to rally their teams around a common purpose and instill a sense of pride in the corporate mission. Building a team in the business world is not unlike what McKissick does by engaging his players and giving them the training and development they need to do the job. Trained and empowered, McKissick's team members carry out the plays they've been taught as they encounter the competition on the field and make adjustments in the moment as circumstances change. In the same way, the role of any leader is to be a mentor—helping others to learn and develop and then stepping back and watching them execute according to a bigger plan while making countless smaller decisions along the way. In McKissick-speak, it is not what you know; it's what the kids know that counts.

In business, you invest when things are not in good shape. When you invest at these times, you take a better position than your competitors. When there is a recession and your competition does not invest, they are giving you the advantage.

—Carlos Slim, entrepreneur, investor,
and the world's richest man

Chapter Seven

CARLOS SLIM:
ENTREPRENEURIAL SPIRIT

When *Forbes* magazine announced its list of the top billionaires in the world for 2010, the person in the number one spot was hardly a well-known name: Carlos Slim Helú. A billionaire with a purposefully low profile, Slim had made his fortune, estimated at $53.5 billion, as an entrepreneur, particularly in telecommunications, in Mexico.[1]

An investor and entrepreneur, Slim built a portfolio of companies across several industries. Yet in our conversation about entrepreneurial leadership, what was most striking about him was his quiet humility. Instead of talking about his own abilities, he was quick to credit his success to the person who influenced him the most: his father, Julian Slim Haddad.

Slim shared the story of his father, a Maronite Christian who immigrated to Mexico from Lebanon in 1902 at the age of fourteen to avoid being drafted into the Ottoman army and to find peace and freedom in Mexico, where his brothers were already living and working. During the Mexican Revolution, Julian, a businessman, partnered with his older brother in a general store, which he then bought from his brother three years later. As the revolution dragged on, he continued investing in his company and saw numerous opportunities to buy when others were panicking, which enabled him to acquire properties for far less than they were worth. His foresight paid off handsomely for his family, particularly when Julian sold just two months before the October 1929 stock market crash. He then invested some of that money in devalued Mexico City real estate.

Carlos Slim followed his father's footsteps and made strides of his own. "I learned from my father that you continue to invest and reinvest in your business—including during crises," explained Slim.

Although Slim was only thirteen when his father died, he still takes to heart the lessons he learned from him. In the 1960s and 1970s, Carlos Slim acquired a soft-drink company in need of a turnaround; he also bought a printing company. In the early 1980s, he bought a large stake in Cigatam, Mexico's second-biggest tobacco company and maker of Marlboro cigarettes in that country. The collapse of oil prices in 1982 plunged Mexico, a major exporter of crude oil, into an economic crisis. When then-president José López Portillo nationalized Mexico's banks, companies were selling on the cheap because of socialist fears. Just like his father, Slim was ready to buy when others sold, laying the foundation for the considerable business empire and fortune it would create.

Slim's vast business holdings stretch well beyond the borders of Mexico. His América Móvil telecommunications company also operates related businesses and networks throughout Latin America. During the financial crisis of 2008–2009, Slim invested in assets across North America. For example, he infused $250 million in The New York Times Company when it was beleaguered by high debt, making him an important shareholder. The day of our meeting, *The New York Times* announced quarterly earnings. Hearing the news, a smile curled slowly across Slim's face. Once again, he had invested well.

Although Slim topped the *Forbes* billionaires list, ahead of Bill Gates and Warren Buffett, wealth, as an end in itself, does not seem to motivate or interest him. Throughout our conversation wealth was discussed only in conceptual terms, not as it related to him personally. In plain words, he did not talk about what it was like to be the world's richest man. More to the point, he did not show it.

Slim's office in Mexico City was large but by no means ostentatious. Like the man himself, who came to our interview carrying a tie he was about to put on and with a simple Swiss Army watch strapped on his wrist, his office was obviously geared for working and not to impress. The most dominant features were floor-to-ceiling bookcases filled with volumes, evidence that Slim is a voracious reader, particularly of history. With the mind of a scholar, he is a self-disciplined, lifelong learner committed to a scientific, mathematical approach.

When Slim said his house is not as nice as the one he grew up in, the juxtaposition of humility and pride in his voice was striking. He took great pride in his simple lifestyle, which he attributed to his "education and conviction." Hunger only for material things, he believes, is a sign of weakness, a character flaw. "When you don't have money, it is a problem," he said. But an even bigger ill is when people "have money in excess and they are not conducting businesses and making investments, creating jobs, and doing things for society. They are only thinking possessions, possessions. . . ."

The only extravagance in Slim's life is an extensive art collection for which he is building a contemporary museum in Mexico City, the new home of the Soumaya Museum, named after his late wife who died in 1999. In his office, however, there was little evidence of his passion for art other than a few paintings on the wall.

Perhaps the most telling object in Slim's office was a copybook, a ledger of sorts that his father asked Slim to keep when he was only a boy. From his father, Slim had learned about business and investing, including the basics, such as keeping a balance sheet. "My father used to say, 'Make it clean and make it on time,'" Slim described.

Given his success as an entrepreneur, Slim's lessons from his father have clearly served him well.

An Intrepid Investor

Slim thrives on facts and figures. During our conversation, facts and figures seemed to orbit inside Slim's brain as he constructed ratios, compared numbers, and solved equations. He wondered aloud the exact level of GDP Mexico's economy would have to reach in order to take off without the risk of falling back down. He pondered stock prices, asset values, and return on investments.

Clearly, numbers were second nature to Slim, an engineer by training and a former mathematics instructor. In the early 1960s, he was a student at the National Autonomous University of Mexico and also worked as a professor of mathematics in order to support himself. This mathematical gift later helped him to assess under-valued assets and unlock business opportunities.

Although Slim has holdings in multiple industries, his primary field is telecommunications. His Teléfonos de México holds an estimated 79-percent share of the land lines in Mexico. In cellular telephone services, Slim's companies boast a strong and growing market share in Latin America. "We developed the concept of prepay; that was our idea," he said proudly. "We subsidize handsets to make them available to everyone. We are looking for universal service so that everyone can have a mobile phone. We have 85 percent penetration in Latin America and are investing to increase broadband penetration."

Slim's vision is for every consumer to have a mobile telephone and broadband connection. Although that goal is naturally good for business, he also believes in these technologies and their ability to improve the country's productivity. With better productivity comes economic improvement, followed by more job creation.

Although his holdings of more than two hundred companies sometimes draw comparisons with John D. Rockefeller, in many ways Slim brought to mind another billionaire—Warren Buffett, a savvy investor who is constantly on the lookout for solid businesses that are undervalued because of market conditions or other circum-stances. Slim's investments are not without risk. After all, assets are undervalued because of unfavorable conditions or even panic. However, he has been able to invest strategically and in the process build an incredible portfolio of holdings.

"There are moments when things are very low in price that normally are very expensive. In business, you invest when things are not in good shape," Slim explained. "When you invest at these times, you take a better position than your competitors. When there is a recession and your competition does not invest, they are giving you the advantage."

In the aftermath of the global financial crisis, Slim's companies invested a total of more than $3.2 billion in Mexico. If his father had fearlessly invested during the Mexican Revolution, Slim observed rhetorically, "How can I not invest in the crisis?"

Slim's view of investing in a crisis is reflected in the culture of his companies, including his flagship, Grupo Carso, which has diverse holdings across several business sectors, including industrial, commercial, infrastructure and construction, and hospitality. The "ten principles" for Grupo Carso listed on the company's Web site are leadership tenets right out of Slim's life experiences and lessons learned from his father. For example: "Maintain austerity in good times in order to strengthen, capitalize and accelerate the development of the company, and thus avoid bitterly drastic adjustment in times of crisis."[2] In other words, be cautious during bull markets and invest during bear markets.

The lesson for business leaders is to be on the lookout for opportunities when others are ceding ground. As witnessed during the financial crisis, companies with solid balance sheets are able to make strategic acquisitions when times are tough and pay far less than they would at other times. Making that kind of move, however, takes not only fiscal discipline to be prepared, but also a keen understanding of the marketplace. Buying just because a company is undervalued is no bargain. As Slim has demonstrated, victory belongs to the intrepid investor who finds value by monitoring and measuring, and deploys capital strategically when others cannot or will not.

A LEADER OF LEADERS

Slim proudly described himself as more of an entrepreneur than a corporate leader. "In the United States in many of the big businesses, the entrepreneur does not exist. It's the executive," he said. "These leaders are there because they are good executives. But the entrepreneur who founded the company disappeared."

Slim's brand of entrepreneurial leadership is distinguished by the way he delegates authority to the executives who run his businesses day-to-day. In this regard, he acts as a leader of leaders, working closely with a small cadre who oversee his business holdings. "My job is to work with them," he explained.

Slim has retired from most of the boards of his companies and has put his sons Arturo, Daniel, Carlos, Marco Antonio, and Patrick in charge. His primary focus these days is the foundations he leads with Arturo and for which he acts much like the chief investment officer. His entrepreneurial leadership style, however, is still very much in evidence. Slim's companies have a simple organizational structure with few layers. Despite the size and scope of his business holdings, Slim's vision is to maintain the agility of a small company, particularly when it comes to rapid decision making.

By delegating responsibilities, Slim has been able to develop leadership talent internally, which he prefers: homegrown talent that comes through the ranks of the operation knows the business well and understands the culture and values.

Since the 1990s, Slim's operations have grown at a rate of 66 percent per year, making the issue of talent development a critical one. "When you grow so much you have many problems," he admitted. One of them is having a deep-enough bench of people to promote to run business units. To meet that need, managers who are interested in working internationally are selected and groomed for the future. Regardless of age or number of years with the company, if an employee displays promise and ability, he or she will be given the opportunity to rise in the company. "I think the best way to find out anything is to look at what they have done in the past," he said.

Talent development focuses on the skills to get the job done and fosters teams that operate efficiently and effectively. It is as much an art as it is a science. There needs to be a common mind-set among senior management that is grounded in integrity and trust. Simply put, executives must trust each other to do what is right.

In our discussion, what became very apparent was the importance Slim places on adherence to values. "The people inside the group need to have some conditions to follow. We have a philosophy of leadership, ideas, and concepts. They need to share that," he added. "Also, when they get together, groups cannot compete against each other inside the company. We need to go in the same direction—not competing on the inside but competing on the outside."

As Slim sees it, when there is strong talent development in the company, the philosophy and culture of the organization become second nature, which promotes harmony and a cohesive culture. At the same time, the organization cannot be closed off to outsiders who join through recruitment or an acquisition. "You need to have a culture that is flexible, that people can adapt to and would join with pleasure," Slim said.

Whether internally developed or brought from the outside, the team must work and interact in a positive fashion that motivates others. Slim explained, "You cannot have people in your organization who are pessimists. They take you to mediocrity." Rather, he advocated what he called "patient optimism," pursuing opportunities and allowing people enough time to produce the desired results.

The type of alignment of mind and heart that Slim talked about can infuse a culture with creativity. Followers turn to the leader for cues such as believing that a problem can be solved or that a crisis is temporary. When a leader displays confidence and optimism, it becomes infectious and others believe that, despite the challenges, goals can be reached and even exceeded.

Slim also instilled in others the importance of having a purpose beyond one's own accomplishments, a belief that is central to his values. "Work that is done well is not only a responsibility to one's self and to society, it is also an emotional need. You cannot live without doing something; [you need] a direction in life. It's very important for leaders in business to work to create human capital, a team that has the same sense of purpose and alignment. They will feel that they are doing something that is important for society and the people around them. That is very important, along with having achievements," Slim said. "People need to feel very good about their achievements. They get pride from what they are doing."

MEASURE, MONITOR, AND COMPETE

Fundamental to Slim's leadership is an overarching discipline to monitor and measure. With an encyclopedic grasp of details and keen observation skills, Slim appeared to miss nothing. As he looked up figures and circled statistics in a newspaper article, he seemed to buzz with boundless energy. Perhaps it goes back to the days when his father sent him out with a notebook to jot down the prices that competitors were charging for products in their stores. ("I felt like a spy looking at the prices," Slim remembered with a chuckle.)

Slim runs his businesses on targets and benchmarks, from profit margins to market penetration. He analyzes data on other companies and industries, such as the relative valuation of telecommunication stocks. He looks beyond his home market, which he dominates, to the global marketplace for comparison. "You have to have an international reference of competition. You have to have the highest [standards]," he explained. "Think of an athlete. He may be very good in his own house, but not as good as his neighbors. You have to go beyond your home. You have to go worldwide."

The broader lesson for leaders is that measuring and monitoring continually provide a basis, a scorecard if you will, of how well or poorly a business is doing. Unless companies commit to benchmarking—whether division to division, current versus past results, or in comparison to other firms—they cannot truly judge their performance and determine where they can make improvements. For Slim, these practices also help to identify potential opportunities and determine appropriate valuations. Such measurements and targets are a way of life and doing business. Across his holdings he preaches the importance of modernization, growth, and quality. Training is essential to developing talent. Simplification and continuous improvement bolster productivity and competitiveness. By using global benchmarks, businesses become more efficient as costs and expenses are reduced.

THE RESPONSIBILITY OF WEALTH

Given his vast wealth and extensive business holdings, Slim has attracted his share of critics. The principal complaint against him boils down to the fact that he is enormously wealthy while millions of his countrymen live in poverty. Slim countered the criticism with his beliefs about the role of business: that creating wealth and making improvements in society occur largely through employment opportunities. The companies he owns, for example, employ more than two hundred thousand people throughout Latin America.

The idea that poor countries should have low-performing domestic companies, a chronic lack of wealth, and only strong foreign companies is "plain perversity," Slim added. The only way for countries to develop is with strong and competitive domestic companies. "To say that in poor countries there should not be wealthy people and strong companies is like saying that there should not be world-class scientists, engineers, architects, etc. That is [like saying] poor countries should be in poverty forever," Slim argued.

At the same time, he sees wealth not as a privilege but a responsibility. With the creation of wealth comes strategic investment, economic activity, growth, and employment, allowing countries to "break the barrier of underdevelopment."

The first responsibility of wealth, Slim believes, is not to guard it but to create more. Otherwise its positive effects cannot be spread and felt across society, particularly in the fight against poverty and in the development of a middle class. "It is like a fruit tree. You distribute a good part of the fruits, not the branches of the tree, and 'reinvest' part of the fruit seeds to grow more trees and create wealth. Wealth should be created by investing to create more wealth. Income is the fruit of wealth. If you do not do that, you will not have more income," Slim observed. "The more income you have in the economy, the more middle class you will have, the strongest market [will] develop, and the best society develops. I don't believe you need to create wealth first and then distribute wealth. Wealth is created because the market, society, the welfare [of the people], and the economy are growing. . . . Development is sustained and grown with the employment and welfare of the population."

In fact, Slim believes that as a society and its economic systems become more evolved, it is the responsibility of the private sector to encourage further economic activity, promote employment, and reduce poverty. "The government and private sector combined are very important to provide modern and high-quality health and education to fight poverty and all its consequences," he added.

Practicing what he preaches, Slim stepped up his philanthropic activities. In 2007, he announced increased endowments for two of his foundations to $10 billion from $4 billion over the next four years, along with other charitable contributions.[3] His Carlos Slim Institute for Health is aimed at improving health care in Mexico and Latin America. Other endeavors target education and providing opportunities in sports. "Government resources are not enough to solve social or economic problems," he added. "We have to create wealth and employment. . . . The only way you finish with poverty is with jobs. To have better jobs you have to have better education."

You Can't Take It with You

For all the wealth he has built, Slim could be living the high life, and yet he has continued to work hard in his many businesses and foundations. His work ethic and his business empire are his legacy, his gift to the world that he is passing on through his family. Now, with his sons and sons-in-law involved in the business, he has instilled in them the same principles that he learned from his father. It is clear Slim believes that he can do the greatest good through his businesses and foundations. "When I pass away, I will not take one cent. I will not take anything," he said. "[I am] a temporary manager of the wealth."

Slim's interests—mathematics, art, philanthropy, and history—form the measure of the man and engage him. During a philosophical moment, he shared a favorite saying, reciting it first in Spanish and then translating into English: "Impose your will against your weakness."

It is a powerful statement that speaks to emotional control, staying positive instead of giving into negativity, and accepting one's flaws and mistakes and being willing to learn from them. In this one sentence Slim seemed to sum up his outlook on life.

The words also revealed another dimension of the man: his inclination toward lifelong learning. Beyond the numbers and the analytics, the benchmarks and valuations, Slim never stops working on himself to become more self-aware. As a leader, to the best of his ability, he strives to embody principles and values, setting a standard for others.

As an entrepreneur, Slim has pursued opportunities when others shied away, particularly investing in times of crisis. His bold approach has made him incredibly rich, but that has not been the primary motivation. With the disciplined and curious mind of a scientist, Slim has put his theories into action: buying when the competitors were ceding the advantage, finding undervalued assets, and creating wealth that translates into jobs and economic opportunity for others. He saw the big picture but never neglected the small details. Most important, he has demonstrated why monitoring and measuring are key components of leadership, enabling CEOs to keep a watchful eye on the present while planning for the future.

Never did I think of giving up, because of all the employees I was responsible for. Moreover, once I establish a goal, I will never give up until it is reached.

—Liu Chuanzhi, founder and
chairman of the board,
Lenovo Group Ltd.

Chapter Eight

LIU CHUANZHI: PERSEVERANCE

In any entrepreneurial venture, there are fundamental challenges starting with the need to innovate, compete, and grow an idea into a global business. It is a difficult, high-risk journey that few complete successfully. For Liu Chuanzhi, founder of Beijing-based Lenovo Group Ltd., the fourth-largest personal computer manufacturer in the world, there was another far more daunting obstacle, namely, the limitations of China's centrally planned economy during the 1980s when China's government discouraged private enterprise. Despite these monumental challenges and countless setbacks, Liu's tiny computer company, started in 1984 with only eleven employees, grew into a global powerhouse, one that twenty years after its founding stunned the world when it acquired the personal computer business of none other than IBM, the granddaddy of the PC.

At the time of our conversation in August 2010, Liu had returned about a year earlier to the chairmanship of Lenovo. He had retired as chairman in 2005, following the completion of the IBM deal. But when Lenovo, his brainchild, suffered a decline in sales and profitability due to the financial crisis and a reduction in orders from its commercial customers, Liu took on the mission to get the company back on track. He was successful, and Lenovo returned to profitability in 2010.

"When Lenovo suffered a difficulty, I returned in spite of getting older," Liu said through an interpreter, "because this is the business I created with my colleagues."

His return to the company he founded revealed more than just pride of ownership. For Liu, it was also a sign of his perseverance and willingness to go the distance to realize his vision. These are the same distinguishing characteristics that he exhibited from the very beginning. Although there may have been those who doubted the fate of the company, Liu was never one of them. "We started the company from scratch," Liu recalled proudly. "We started the business from nothing. Perhaps, at the beginning, nobody believed that our company could stand for long."

He had always dreamed of the day when the company he started under the name Lian Xiang (it was changed to Lenovo in 2003 to create a more recognizable global brand) would be the IBM of China. At the time, such a plan seemed preposterous. Not only was the company tiny, but this was China in the early 1980s, with a tightly controlled and centrally planned economy, regulations that restricted trade, and an ideology that despised private wealth accumulation. Not exactly an entrepreneur's paradise.

"We were always in fear of some emerging issues. These problems were surely a kind of test," Liu said philosophically.

Yet Liu was persistent, determined to turn an idea into reality. Part of it was commitment, backed by the belief in the technology that he had seen in Chinese research laboratories and wanted to develop into commercial products. After weighing the risks, Liu saw little or no downside. "In China we have a saying, 'The barefoot are not afraid of the dressed ones,'" he said. "So I was 'barefoot' at the time, and I did not worry about failing."

With a vision of what was possible, Liu established a company that became China's largest PC maker and the fastest growing PC manufacturer in the world. In 2010, Lenovo ranked as the world's fourth-largest PC manufacturer with nearly $17 billion in revenues.

Considering where the company started, the outcome seems nearly impossible. A picture of the company's first headquarters reflects its humble beginnings: a tiny building that was formerly used as the front-gate reception room of the state-owned Chinese Academy of Sciences' Computer Institute. Yet that tiny, nondescript building proved to house a powerful incubator of ideas.

GRAND PLANS FROM A HUMBLE BEGINNING

Seated in a conference room at Lenovo's modern headquarters in Beijing, Liu looked the part of the executive-statesman who has represented his company, his industry, and his country well. Although he has won numerous accolades and awards and received international recognition, Liu, who is known as the "godfather of China's information industries,"[1] resolutely dismissed any notion of being a born leader, considering himself rather ordinary before his company was created.

"I had no such great aspirations and vision twenty-six years ago when I started my business. . . . I was forty years old at the time. I did not know my capabilities as a leader. Before then, I thought of myself as very common and nothing special. But then I developed gradually," he observed.

He then shared his early life experiences, which shed light on his intense determination.

As a young man, Liu had dreamed of becoming a fighter pilot and distinguished himself as the only candidate from his class at school to be considered for training. Although his father was a member of the Communist Party, one of Liu's relatives was a "rightest," which made Liu unfit for duty. Devastated by the loss of his dream, Liu was consoled by his father who said, "No matter what you do in the future, whether it's great or just something ordinary, so long as you are an upright human being you will be my good son."[2] For Liu, his father's words were more than just encouragement. They set the standard for the kind of leader that Liu would strive to become.

Enrolled in the Xi'an Military Communications Engineering Institute in 1961, Liu studied radar, which gave him an introduction to computers. After graduation, he was sent to work at a research institute in Chengdu under the country's defense department where his first assignment was to study captured American radar systems to improve Chinese radar. Although he did not know it at the time, Liu was being given an entrée to technology, a field in which he would later distinguish himself as an entrepreneur. Before any of those hopes or dreams could take root, however, Liu would face two brutal years of forced labor during the Cultural Revolution.

Liu was among the many professionals and intellectuals who were persecuted and forced to do manual labor. In 1968, Liu was sent to a rice farm, performing back-breaking toil to plant rice seedlings on a commune. Later, he was moved to a farm where political prisoners and those whom the government wanted to "reform" through hard labor had been sent.[3] Despite all that he endured, Liu said nothing during our interview about his own circumstances. His only allusions were his comments about his country during a time of turmoil when China was "in the midst of class struggle and the people were undergoing hardships."

In 1970, Liu was allowed to return to his field of research and went to the Computer Institute under the Chinese Academy of Sciences where he worked as an engineer-administrator. Although conditions were certainly better there than at the rice farm, Liu faced other hardships. His work focused on magnetic data storage, but no one had the desire to turn such technology into products. "Some scientific and technological achievements I made were put on the shelf," Liu remembered.

Liu seemed far from fulfilling his dream. Rather than being stymied, however, Liu turned his unhappiness into a motivating force to instigate change in his life. Like many leaders who find themselves at a crossroads of choice, Liu charted his own way to what was possible by seizing opportunities as they arose.

Following Mao's death and economic reforms established by his successor Deng Xiaoping, China began to be more open to entrepreneurs who wanted to establish their own companies. Realizing that here, at last, was his chance to explore his ideas, Liu decided to try his hand at the computer business. "I had a strong impulse to make something," he explained. "I wanted to know what I could do."

Liu convinced ten colleagues to join him in establishing a tiny computer company with the equivalent of only $25,000 in initial capital from the Chinese Academy of Sciences. "The capital was very limited and far from being enough to establish an enterprise, which normally would require several million dollars or tens of millions of yuan," Liu explained. "Nevertheless, we were intent upon making our computers. So we were forced to open up a new road."

Following that road proved to be quite a journey because Liu and his company straddled two worlds: those of a fledgling technology firm that longed to become a global brand and a homegrown Chinese enterprise that was controlled by the state.

STRADDLING TWO WORLDS

Long before there was Lenovo the global company, there was Lian Xiang, a Chinese start-up. Although the company would eventually become one of China's first publicly traded firms, with shares listed on the Hong Kong Stock Exchange, Lian Xiang was state-owned because of seed money from the Chinese Academy of Sciences. As the leader, Liu faced a constant balancing act between doing what was good for the company and remaining loyal to the Chinese government. He faced numerous investigations by the Chinese government over the years to see if he had committed any "economic crimes," in effect, acting too much like the head of a private enterprise. "In order for someone to do well in business in China, he must be concerned about the economy, the politics, and the [political] philosophy," Liu observed.

For Liu, these challenges severely tested his patience and his perseverance, and even caused health problems such as chronic insomnia. Yet never did he look back and wish that he had stayed on the research career track where a promotion and a raise in pay would have been ensured. Even when several other new Chinese companies failed, Liu was determined that both he and Lian Xiang would survive the challenges. "Never did I think of giving up, because of all the employees I was responsible for. Moreover, once I establish a goal, I will never give up until it is reached," he said.

In the beginning, the constraints of a planned economy were formidable obstacles. Lian Xiang wanted to manufacture PCs, but without a license from the Chinese government it could not open a factory. Instead, the company started out as a distributor for foreign companies whose products were just beginning to penetrate the Chinese market. Lian Xiang began manufacturing computer motherboards in Hong Kong, and when the products became successful, Chinese authorities granted the company a license to manufacture computers in China.

Whenever a problem arose, Liu found a solution. The dual talents of entrepreneur and problem solver are both admirable and necessary. Leaders in any field cannot rely on a vision or an idea. They must also be able to execute and implement a strategy, making adjustments—even dramatic ones—whenever circumstances change or problems arise.

Other significant hurdles posed by China's state-controlled economy included controls on the price of all goods. Lian Xiang wanted to price its Chinese character card for computers at RMB2,000 (equivalent to about $300 today) each. However, the government's commodity pricing agency determined they should only charge RMB200 (about $30). "They fixed the price based on the cost of raw materials and components, and then added 20 percent. They did not consider the labor [to develop the product]. Therefore, we had to discuss and plead with them. It was very difficult," Liu said.

Lian Xiang achieved several notable accomplishments, made all the more satisfying because of the difficulties that the company had endured just to survive. For example, in 1988, its Chinese-character card system, which enabled computers to process Chinese characters, received the National Science-Technology Progress Award in China.

For every achievement, however, there was another obstacle. In order to import computer components, Lian Xiang needed access to foreign exchange. Unable to tap government sources, the company had to resort to the black market. "We had no other means except to use such an operation," Liu said. "It seemed that there was a line, and you may have to violate the law if you crossed the line. But if you stayed behind the line, you would not move forward."

Given the government restrictions at the time, Liu saw no other choice but to skirt overly oppressive rules that otherwise would have killed the enterprise.

KNOW YOUR INDUSTRY

After successfully managing the obstacles in China, Lian Xiang faced new challenges, this time from the West. For the first six years of the company's existence, China restricted foreign firms through high tariffs and the need for government approvals to do business. In the early 1990s, China relaxed its regulations and allowed a freer flow of trade. In response, foreign firms, including computer companies, flocked to China. Although the price of foreign-made computers was higher compared with Chinese machines, so was the quality. Rather than acquiesce, Liu decided to study the foreign competition and learn from them.

"We occupied only 2 percent of the market in China at that time," Liu recalled. "As we competed with the foreign enterprises, we made an in-depth and complete study of the PC industry, such as how to develop the market, how to reduce costs, how to control bad debt, and so forth."

As stated in previous chapters, learning agility and adjustive leadership are powerful prerequisites for success. Liu exhibited both of these qualities as he set forth a plan to gain in-depth industry knowledge from Western competitors. From Hewlett-Packard, for which Lian Xiang was a distributor, it learned how to market and organize its sales channels. From Intel and Microsoft, Lian Xiang learned how Western technology companies operated. This strategy reflects one of Liu's prime lessons in leadership: know your industry. Unless leaders and their teams understand every facet of the business—technology advances, customer demands, and competitors' strategies—they cannot compete effectively.

Although all industries face change, in technology it is endemic. Computers have become faster, more powerful, and cheaper at an astounding rate. Liu has compared technology products to fresh fruit: sell them now or they will quickly lose their value. Lian Xiang sought to gain a competitive edge by innovating. By 1996, it boasted the highest market share for PCs in China for the first time and also introduced its first branded laptop computer. Needing to reduce its component costs, Lian Xiang entered into negotiations with industry giants, such as Intel. Although its scale was too small to have much negotiating power, Lian Xiang was able to improve its supply chain, cut costs, and reduce prices, which boosted its sales. The move was symbolic as well as strategic. Under Liu's leadership, Lian Xiang's supply chain efficiency made it more like a multinational company than a Chinese firm that typically was more concerned about tariffs or foreign exchange risk.

With a thorough understanding of the PC business not only in China but also globally, the company now known as Lenovo was ready for a bold move: purchasing the IBM PC business for $1.75 billion. At the time the deal was announced in December 2004, *The New York Times* observed that Lenovo was "emblematic of the ambitions of emergent Chinese industrial giants to create global brands and capture market share beyond their own borders."[4] In China, the deal was likened to a snake swallowing an elephant because Lenovo's revenues at the time were less than 25 percent of those for the IBM unit and its ThinkPad brand.

In the years since acquiring the IBM PC business, Lenovo has continued to expand its own branded products and entered into new ventures. It broke into the emerging mobile Internet area through LePhone, its answer to Apple's iPhone. LePhone was launched first in the Chinese market and will expand elsewhere as the product becomes established. The new product is the result of the work of Lenovo's R&D teams based in China, the United States, and Japan—what Liu called "technology accumulation." The company plans to roll out another mobile Internet product, LePad, a tablet PC, in 2011. Although Lenovo has faced some criticism for a lack of new product innovation, Liu described the company's cautious approach. "The Chinese have a saying: 'Think seriously before acting.' If you do not, you may fail or be eliminated," he added. As he sees it, innovation must be balanced with careful planning to avoid costly product failures. "We accumulate the capital, seek the goal, and advance toward it firmly," Liu said. "You must think things over to avoid being eliminated."

THE LENOVO WAY

Over the years as Lian Xiang became Lenovo and the company grew into the largest computer manufacturer in China and then in all of Asia, its culture has been a constant. Liu calls it the "Lenovo Way." From the beginning, he established a culture in which he and his team were united in the pursuit of common goals. "People tend to seek their own self-interests. Instead, they should [place] their own interests after the interests of the enterprise," Liu said. "The corporate culture of Lenovo is to make the company the first priority." Lenovo instilled this culture by the way it hires, promotes, and compensates employees so that when the company does well people are rewarded. "The development of the enterprise should be consistent with everyone's pursuits," Liu explained. "If we run the business successfully, it will be more profitable, which will be good for the staff."

The culture is also people-oriented, recognizing the contribution of each individual toward the achievement of the organization's goals. Throughout our discussion, Liu emphasized the importance of developing the team, which he sees as the primary responsibility of the leader. In an interview for the book *The Lenovo Affair*, Liu used an interesting metaphor to describe the people at Lenovo, comparing them to pearls. "Some people are like pearls," Liu said. "And some are not—they can't glow with their own beauty."[5]

Tellingly, Liu did not describe himself as a pearl but rather as the string—the one who assembles the pearls into a necklace. Leadership is not about the person at the top but rather about the organization and what can be achieved when a talented team is brought together, united by a common purpose, and directed by a leader with vision.

Another element of Lenovo's culture is to "be truth seeking and pragmatic," Liu explained. "Actually, this has two meanings: my subordinate cannot cheat me and vice versa. For example, the monthly budget statement cannot contain something false. Furthermore, our external commitment must be credible. We cannot promise something that we cannot accomplish. Hence, 'we do what we say' or 'deliver one's commitment' is paramount at Lenovo." This is a challenge for many leaders, to move beyond what people say they can or will do to what is actually accomplished. The objective is a "say/do ratio" of one-to-one—what is promised is actually delivered.

One of the promises Liu made to the organization was to reward employees by giving them an ownership stake. The problem, however, was that doing so would be nothing short of criminal because the company held what were considered public assets. Through an arrangement Liu devised with the Chinese Academy of Sciences, a portion of the profits were allocated into a fund, the Employee Shareholding Society. Capital was accumulated until 2000 when, with a favorable change in government policies, shares were purchased outright from the government and distributed to employees.

The next step was to figure out how to distribute the shares. Fortunately, Liu had already developed a plan back in 1993, even though the stock would not be purchased for another eight years. Liu's tremendous foresight paid off. "In 1993, when we made the plan, nobody cared about it because they never thought it would come true," Liu added. Liu himself only received 2 percent of the stock, which he believed was a good example of the fairness of the plan.

A SENSE OF PURPOSE

With all that has been accomplished at Lenovo, there is no doubt that Liu has a strong competitive spirit. Outside of business, Liu shows that competitive drive in his passion for soccer. "I was crazy about playing [the sport] in college," he recalled.

As he talked about his enthusiasm for the game, Liu made several observations about what he saw as the ideal coach: one who has "strong willpower" and who "refuses to concede defeat," but who also has a "big heart" to understand his players. The coach must be able to pick the star players and also develop the team, with rules that apply equally to all, which speaks to Liu's leadership approach of working with "collective wisdom and concerted efforts." He recognizes and rewards individuals, but the whole of the organization is what matters the most.

During a visit to the company's headquarters, the sense of collaborative spirit was strong at Lenovo with its nine-person top leadership team. Four of the group members were Chinese, and the rest were from other countries. "They represent all the important functions in the company, and together provide a complete understanding of the industry and the overall economic and political situation, and then make decisions together," Liu said. "We hold many meetings to eliminate misunderstandings and to analyze the current situations so that much more information can be incorporated into our decision making."

In its twenty-six years of existence, the company now known as Lenovo achieved significant milestones, from making its first computer under its own brand to the IBM PC deal. For all Lenovo has achieved, Liu's greatest accomplishment as an entrepreneur has been the sense of purpose he has established for himself and for others.

"Some people are happy because of their wealth—a big home, lots of possessions. Others are happy because of making great [philanthropic] contributions to society, like Warren Buffett and Bill Gates. . . . As for me, I will be happy if my colleagues and subordinates get better development and opportunities," Liu observed. "They will grow the business and through that make great contributions to society. This is my pursuit in life. This is what makes me happy."

For Liu, who persevered through numerous personal and professional hardships to realize his goal, determining one's own purpose and providing opportunities for others are the best reward yet.

First, you're not here to take advantage but rather to add. Second, you will not finish. Third, it is very important that the overall vision of what is being built be shared by several people over time.

—Daniel Vasella, MD; chairman,
Novartis AG

Chapter Nine

DANIEL VASELLA: SELF-AWARENESS

For fourteen years, as chairman and CEO of Novartis AG, Daniel Vasella, MD, led the Swiss pharmaceutical company through a period of rapid growth with carefully chosen acquisitions, mergers, divestitures, and investments, including in a world-class research facility. Under Vasella's leadership, Novartis developed a diversified portfolio: pharmaceuticals to treat cardiovascular disease, cancer, and other conditions; generic drugs; vaccines; and consumer health products. He also pioneered initiatives to ensure access to medicines, particularly in poorer areas of the world, to treat diseases such as malaria and leprosy. Such distinctions have led Vasella to be honored for his leadership within the pharmaceutical industry and the European business community overall, including being named the *Financial Times's* most influential European businessman of the past quarter century.[1]

Vasella, who retired as CEO of Novartis in January 2010 but continues as an active chairman of the company, has distinguished himself in another way as well. He has a unique background as both a corporate leader and a physician. Although Vasella has not practiced medicine for more than twenty years, he still identifies closely with the medical profession. As the head of the third-largest pharmaceutical company in the world, he has had an effect on tens of millions of patients worldwide. "Now, I haven't invented a single drug myself but I know that I was able to make sure that some drugs were big successes for the patients and the company," Vasella said. "I am most proud of the medicines we were able to deliver to patients that improved the way medicine is being practiced—in cancer, in ophthalmology—and that changed the lives of people."

His medical background has also enhanced his leadership in business, imparting the analytical abilities to diagnose problems and determine paths to solutions. "From a point of view of analytics, they are not very different. In medicine you try to understand the condition, look at the symptoms, identify the underlying causes, and then you try to intervene—optimally to change or remove the cause or otherwise to treat symptomatically. It's not very different in business," he observed.

Likewise, in business as in medicine there must be well-trained teams at the ready who understand the mission and the purpose, what they are expected to do, and who is in charge. "It isn't so dramatic in business as it is in the hospital emergency room, but the principle is the same," Vasella added.

Known for being an empathetic listener, Vasella was the kind of physician who understood the heightened emotions that underlie any difficult or traumatic situation, which he himself first encountered as a young patient. As a child, Vasella was sick with asthma, tuberculosis, and meningitis and spent more than a year in a hospital and a sanitarium. "I had terrible physicians and fantastic physicians. The difference was not so much technical knowledge but the way they dealt with me: how they explained what they would be doing, how they took away or augmented my fear," he recalled.

Vasella endured emotional losses as a youngster, as well: an older sister died of cancer when he was ten, and his father passed away of complications from surgery when Vasella was thirteen. Vasella has credited his sister's fight against her illness for his own interest in medicine. Vasella, who is Swiss and speaks three languages fluently, went to the University of Bern Medical School, which he attended with another sister, who later died in an accident. After graduating from medical school in 1979, Vasella worked in pathology and internal medicine and eventually became chief resident at the university.

Because of his personal experiences during his own illnesses and the deaths of family members, Vasella was able to relate to his patients on a deep level, particularly when they shared their emotions. "The depth of the soul is much deeper and more complex than what people will tell you," he said. "When they are sick, when they are dying, people may tell you things that they never told anybody. You may see character traits and fears that you normally don't see."

In 1988 Vasella joined Swiss drug company Sandoz Pharma, where he rose through the ranks from product manager for an anti–pancreatic cancer drug to eventually become CEO of Sandoz in 1994. When Sandoz and another Swiss pharmaceutical company, Ciba-Geigy, merged to form Novartis in 1996, Vasella was named CEO.

After he left medical practice, Vasella brought with him valuable insight into human nature, especially knowledge of the fears and self-doubts that people harbor deep inside. As he witnessed countless times, even in business interactions an array of emotions are felt and processed, often below the surface and at times unconsciously. These emotions have the power to influence perceptions, decisions, behaviors, and interactions with others, positively or negatively. "These emotions are there, even if people are very self-controlled," Vasella said. "You don't ever want to force anybody to disclose something that they don't want to disclose, but you are ready and not afraid if they do."

Although self-awareness is recognized to be a strategic leadership skill, as a leader Vasella seemed to take it to a higher level. During our conversation he shared his views on the importance of self-awareness and spoke candidly about his own development needs over the years.

THE SELF-AWARE LEADER

Empathy was a quality Vasella brought to the corporate world. A less-developed trait in the beginning was "aggressiveness, in the sense of being direct and candid," Vasella described. By the time he became CEO, however, Vasella discovered he had become too demanding at times and was perceived by subordinates as being hard to satisfy. "Early on in my CEO career, people said I didn't praise enough and I was too tough. So I asked myself to what degree it was true and not true," he added. "And it was true. I was very good at finding what wasn't good enough and so there was a certain level of constant dissatisfaction with performance. Of course, when we had a success there was also a deep satisfaction, but it never lasted for long."

Vasella realized he needed balance between having empathy and expecting excellence. He observed, "I think both sides have to be well developed so that you have periods of listening, of being able to imagine the feelings and thinking of others, but then also the ability to distance yourself and ask what the situation requires and to demand it."

Vasella sought insights into what motivated people to achieve goals and even exceed expectations. Not surprisingly the motivations were mostly intrinsic, not extrinsic. "People will go beyond what they think is possible if they find the objective is interesting and challenging," he said. "If they think they can make it, but aren't entirely sure, they need support across the organization."

With strong and capable people in place, the team will improve even further, bolstered by a culture of self-awareness, collaboration, and mutual respect. As Vasella succinctly explained, "Good and great people attract better people."

The process starts with the leader. In Vasella's case, he employed his skills and expertise in emotional intelligence to build a culture and an organization that puts its values first. For example, to foster collaboration and reduce bureaucracy, Novartis changed its physical working environment to one with more open spaces. On a different level, Vasella added another component to the culture, which he called "the stories we tell," the shared experiences within the company that reflect a greater purpose than just the bottom line. "These are the stories we can tell about what we did, not just for profit, but also that we helped to save hundreds of thousands of lives by providing drugs for malaria or other drugs at no profit," he observed. "It is real life—real events, real decisions."

A self-aware leader can not only inspire people, but also help them see where they are falling short of their potential. Once again, this starts with the leader, who must mirror for the team certain behaviors, such as setting an example for how to rise above the human tendency to wallow in negative emotions such as anger, self-pity, and blame. "We all face—during a career, during a week, and even during the day sometimes—moments of frustration, dissatisfaction, anger, you name it. We need to be able to overcome that, to live with it and contain it. I think a very important ability for a leader is to be able to do containment: to take in negative feelings and actions of others without passing them along and not react to them without reflecting." A common excuse, "It's not me, it's my boss," is "the typical pattern of people who cannot act as containers of negative feelings and as buffers in some way," he explained.

If people never develop the ability to reduce their emotionally charged reactions to certain people or situations, Vasella believes they will never reach their full potential no matter how intelligent or skilled they may be. "When they feel threatened or they feel frustrated, they come back to past patterns and beliefs and they become prisoners of their own history," he added. "I think it's very important that people have enough ability to observe themselves and say, 'It's strange. Each time somebody says XYZ, I am getting aggressive or depressed and I do XYZ. Why am I doing this? Because it is not what I should be doing.' If people don't have the ability to introspect, then I believe they are less able to really perform well."

Too often in companies, the tendency is to ignore the emotional undercurrents out of fear of creating an even bigger problem or conflict. Instead the opposite happens. A one-time event becomes an endemic problem that undermines the culture, the morale, and ultimately the performance of the team. It takes courage on the part of a leader to be willing to address difficult issues involving someone's behavior or negative attitude. By doing so, however, the leader is able to raise the other person's awareness and give him or her a chance to change.

"I have sat down with managers who had been disrespectful with subordinate support staff and told them, 'If I ever see you behaving this way again I will fire you, even if you have the best results. You don't do this. It sets such a bad example,'" Vasella said. The most important measure for people's behavior, he added, is not the way they treat their boss or important customers. Rather, "how they deal with the weakest and the lowest in the organization. So if I saw something that is inappropriate, I was very direct in dealing with it. Generally, people understand."

When a leader extends common courtesy to others, that positive influence permeates the organization. Respect becomes the standard, the expected behavior from leader to followers and among the entire team.

At the same time, in order to protect and nurture the culture, a leader must discern when someone is not a fit, even when that person is someone whom the leader has hired. "If they don't fit, you have to undo what you have done," Vasella explained. "You have to have the courage to say, 'This is the wrong person.' And I have fired people whom I have selected before at the risk of having people say about me, 'He is not logical. Why does he do that?' The thing is, if I made these decisions too early, people didn't understand. And if I made them too late, they said, 'Well, finally. He is too slow in acting.' Choosing the right timing in making personnel appointments and changes is very important."

Like the other leaders interviewed, Vasella admitted to making his share of mistakes over the years, such as a new hire that did not turn out as planned. Even with mistakes that made him embarrassed, Vasella used his emotional maturity to learn from the experience instead of trying to distance himself from it as soon as possible. "You don't learn as much from successes as from mistakes, which of course means you have to be willing to admit that you make mistakes. How do you do that without losing self-assurance?" he remarked.

His answer was that people who are self-aware accept and reconcile the contradictory aspects of their personalities: having weaknesses yet being confident, having empathy but being able to be aggressive, being understanding and forgiving and also being demanding. "You may have many aspects that are seemingly contradictory," he observed. "It's a question of breadth and judgment."

TAKING RISKS

Looking back on his fourteen-year tenure as CEO of Novartis, Vasella described leading the company through significant changes: divesting chemicals, agribusiness, and nutrition; entering other businesses such as vaccines and diagnostics; and expanding in pharmaceuticals and building the second-largest generic business in the world. He also spoke of the company's track record of discovering, developing, and launching innovative medicines. "It's a higher number than anyone else in the industry," he said proudly.

In a research and development–intensive business, however, successes come only after an astounding failure rate. "In R&D, in the beginning of our process, we lose 90 percent of the products. When we are down the road, seven to ten years, we still lose 30 percent of the products," Vasella explained. "There is no way around it: we succeed less often than we fail."

As CEOs well know, the ability to face, accept, and learn from failure is a prerequisite for leadership. As every leader has described, failure is unavoidable. The only remedy is to control the downside. "You have to be willing to learn how you can minimize the impact of failure," Vasella offered.

The key for leaders is to understand the risks they're facing, to identify the downside if things do not work out as planned and the potential gain if they do, and then to decide whether or not to move forward. Keeping the status quo, however, is never an option. The goal, though, should not be to do away with risk. In fact, Vasella said that taking no risk may be the biggest risk of all. Simply put, if a company doesn't take any risks, it can't make any money. "Just staying inert in a moving world is crazy," Vasella added. "You cannot do that."

In his role as CEO, Vasella took big risks at times, such as moving the company's global research headquarters from Switzerland to Cambridge, Massachusetts, in May 2002 to establish the Novartis Institutes for BioMedical Research (NIBR). The center directs the company's international network of research operations in places such as the United States, Switzerland, England, Austria, and Italy.

In addition, the company's new head of research came from academia, a departure from past practice. "It was a big change, a big disruption," Vasella recalled. "But I knew that continuing on the path that we were on would not lead to success because science had evolved and the talent pool was not necessarily where we had our headquarters. It was high risk, but we succeeded."

At the time of our conversation in late summer 2010, Novartis had also begun building a large R&D center in Shanghai, where it intends to employ more than one thousand people. "That's a big bet on various fronts: on the political front, the IP [intellectual property] front, and on the investment front," Vasella added. "And these are the bets one takes, but they are rational bets."

When leaders take bold action, they must be comfortable with shouldering the accountability that comes with the decision. The proverbial buck stops at the CEO's office. All a leader can do is deal with the uncertainty and try to make others comfortable with it as well.

"First of all, you can never ensure the outcome. That's why the selection of the people is most important," Vasella explained. He gave the example of when the NIBR in Cambridge was launched and the company received thousands of applications from potential job candidates. "So we could choose very carefully whom we wanted to hire," he added. "And because these are high-tech jobs, the person who did the hiring had to understand what the people were talking about. A high level of competence was needed."

Second, the plan and the strategy have to be rational and able to be explained coherently so that others can understand. "If it's so complex that you don't understand or can't explain it, then it's probably not the right strategy," Vasella continued.

Next, it is essential to manage expectations for when results will be achieved. As any leader knows, one of the worst things to do is to overpromise in terms of results or time frame. The truth may be an uncomfortable message to deliver, but a leader must have the courage and integrity to stand by the facts.

Once again, Vasella turned to an example at the NIBR. The board asked Vasella when the company would know if the center would pay off; he cautioned that it would be five years. "I told them, 'We can see if we are making progress, if the arrows are pointing in the right direction, but please don't expect any results before five years.'" At first the board was surprised—perhaps even a bit shocked. But Vasella maintained his conviction of telling them the uncomfortable truth instead of what they wished to hear. "In biomedical research you need time to show solid results that matter," he added. Fortunately, after five years, as the first biomedical compounds came out of the Cambridge center, Novartis knew it had a winner.

There are other risks that leaders face on a different front: stakeholders and would-be influencers of corporate policy, including politicians, nongovernmental organizations (NGOs), activists, the financial community, including analysts, shareholders, and the media—even partners with which the company does business. "It's a diverse group. In these situations you are exposed to these people who are trying to exert pressure on you as the CEO. They want to influence you to follow their agenda," Vasella said. In order to withstand this pressure, CEOs must be very clear—particularly with the board and within the company—about the organization's purpose, values, goals, and strategies.

"You need to understand the stakeholders, but you don't give in if you don't share their views," he cautioned. "It's a big mistake to be politically correct. You need the courage to be politically incorrect and not popular. The CEO's job is not to win a popularity contest. It is about producing results in the short, medium, and long term; to build a future in which others can continue to grow the company and deliver products to the customers. If you start to make all kinds of concessions, you basically have a strategy *du jour*, when you change the menu based on what someone else wants. That is not going to work."

Ultimately it is up to the leader to own the vision and the strategy to carry it out. Although the ideal is to achieve harmony across the organization and with various stakeholders, the leader needs to keep the greater purpose and long-term objectives in view and accept occasional conflicts. "In the end, as the leader, you are accountable," Vasella added. "Frankly, if you are not, then you are not doing your job and you should not be in that job."

STEWARDSHIP

Although Vasella was credited with the dynamic growth at Novartis, he was clear that the accomplishments achieved during his leadership were part of a continuum, encompassing those who came before him at predecessor companies and those who will follow at Novartis.

This is the essence of corporate stewardship, recognizing that one's leadership is part of a greater whole, with the inherent responsibility of turning the organization over to the next leader who will build on the past and achieve even more.

To illustrate this point, Vasella shared a story told to him by a friend who visited a vineyard in California. As the man admired the property he asked the owner how much it would cost. The vineyard owner answered that it would be impossible to put a price on it. Pointing to a stone wall, the owner explained how his grandfather had started building it and then his father added to it as did he. "I found this to be a fascinating analogy," Vasella said. "It's like no great cathedral was built in one generation."

The same goes for a company, particularly one with a long history like Novartis. (The oldest of its antecedents dates back to 1758.) "There are several implications," Vasella reflected. "First, you're not here to take advantage but rather to add. Second, you will not finish. Third, it is very important that the overall vision of what is being built be shared by several people over time."

As a steward of the company, Vasella recognized that one of his biggest contributions would be a successful succession. Although his departure from the CEO job while retaining the chairmanship in January 2010 was a surprise, Vasella said he had started thinking about the transition as early as 2008.

The process began, he said, by separating governance from potential candidates. In other words, Vasella asked board members to consider first the governance model they wanted to put in place: for example, splitting the chairman and CEO roles, appointing a chief operating officer, and so forth. The criteria for the model were the current and projected challenges for the company and what was needed to continue strong leadership. After the model was determined, then the "people discussion" followed and a successor was selected. Joseph Jimenez, who joined the company in 2007, took over as CEO in February 2010.

With nearly a decade and a half as the top executive, Vasella's tenure was long by comparison with the trend at many companies in which the CEO may serve only a few years. "If people stay two or three years in the job, it's worthless. They should stay at least seven years so that they have a full cycle for what they are doing, although that does depend a little bit on the industry. They need to see the results of their decisions and actions, positive and negative," he explained.

At some point the time will come for the CEO to step down. In Vasella's case, he determined the timing himself when, at age fifty-six with a succession plan finalized, he decided it was time to go. "The transition, of course, is easier if you do it yourself rather than having it done to you," he observed.

Nonetheless, the transition out of the role of the CEO who runs the company day-to-day into a more strategic oversight position as chairman has not always been easy. The challenges he experienced were not the ones he expected. "I anticipated that it would be difficult to pass along the baton and the responsibility and decision power. It wasn't difficult at all; that was easy," he said. "But what was really challenging in the first few months was confronting the question, 'Why am I here?'"

Ever self-aware, Vasella recognized that the root of his discomfort was the fact that throughout his career he had always been given more responsibility and greater accountability. "Suddenly, there was less. And the question became, 'Am I still satisfied?'" In the few months since his shift in roles, the answers have been positive. Instead of burying his emotional discomfort in distraction, he faced it head on and sought the advice of others, such as a friend who had been the head of a large U.S. university and encountered many of the same experiences during his transition. "So it seems that it's part of a normal digestion process," Vasella added.

Now that he is no longer CEO, Vasella has gained perspective that enables him to offer advice to other leaders. Top of his list was the importance of keeping a distinction between one's identity and job title. The challenge, however, is that during one's tenure as CEO the job is all consuming, involving "caring a lot about the company, its people, its products, and the customers you serve," Vasella explained. "Although it is necessary for CEOs to identify themselves with their organizations, it is equally important to be able to step back and separate yourself from your role." This allows leaders to maintain perspective. "You think that what people are telling you is because of who you are and not because you are the CEO," Vasella said. "It's not true. It's because you are the CEO. It's very important to keep a balance. The question is, how do you balance a highly professionalized style of life and everything that you are getting through that position—the power and the money—so that you don't become its first victim?"

One's family can be very helpful in keeping perspective, Vasella shared, because "they should see you as a person and not as a function. And the kids can tell you what weaknesses you have," he added with a chuckle.

Highly self-aware and empathic, Vasella built a corporate culture based on values as well as performance. His thinking and behaviors that also influenced others are perhaps his greatest legacy to the company he helped to build. He instilled a culture of mutual respect in which teams collaborate to take calculated risks to increase innovation and discovery.

I've learned from history that so much of leadership is helping people deal with change and understand how change happens. History is about the nature of change.
—Drew Gilpin Faust, scholar; historian; president, Harvard University

Chapter Ten

DREW GILPIN FAUST:
CATALYST

As the twenty-eighth president of Harvard University, Drew Gilpin Faust made history in 2007 when she became the first woman to lead this Ivy League university, the oldest institution of higher learning in the United States. A noted scholar, history professor, and author of six books on the American Civil War and the South, Faust had come to Harvard six years earlier to be the first dean of its Radcliffe Institute for Advanced Study. At the time, ascending to the presidency of Harvard was the furthest thing from her mind.

"No way!" she said emphatically, recalling that when she arrived Lawrence Summers was president of Harvard. Faust had assumed Summers would hold that position for most of her career. When Summers resigned in 2006 (he later became one of President Obama's economic advisors), Harvard installed an interim leader while searching for a permanent replacement. In February 2007, Faust was chosen. As nearly every leader interviewed told us, opportunities are often unexpected and realized only with a willingness to recognize and pursue them.

When we spoke in early September 2010, Faust was three years into her presidency and had become known for being a catalyst of organizational change: breaking down barriers and silos between academic disciplines and increasing collaboration across the many schools at Harvard. These changes have been in response, at least in part, to the effect of the global financial crisis, which delivered a major blow to the Harvard Endowment, reducing it by 27 percent.[1]

For any leader in business, government, or academics, times of crisis are what ultimately define one's leadership. Although Faust is a scholar by trade, she has clearly learned lessons of leadership from history and risen to the challenges presented to her. She pulled together a team of the great minds in business and finance at Harvard, to whom she gives much credit for contributing their expertise and support during the financial crisis. On her watch as university president, Faust also decided to consider the deeper, more fundamental issues regarding how Harvard operates. "The crisis has given us some opportunities to confront the needed changes and ask the big questions that maybe wouldn't have been on the agenda. Those questions range from how do we do things at Harvard, how are we organized, and how do we operate the university to what is the role of higher education in the world at large."

Looking back, Faust acknowledged the effect that outside forces and unforeseen events have had on her leadership. Responding to an unprecedented global financial crisis was certainly not what anyone envisioned when Faust was selected as president of the university. Yet she drew both inspiration and perspective from the words of Abraham Lincoln, who said, "Events have made me." Although some scholars interpret that quote as a diminishment of Lincoln, that he believed he was a passive recipient of circumstances rather than a great leader, she interpreted his words differently. "Any life is an intersection of events and character and capacity, and of course events make all of us," she observed. "But you also make events. And there is this intersection between who you are and what the world offers you."

Faust also found lessons from the Civil War, which she described as a compressed period of change that brought about dramatic shifts in several dimensions in American life, such as the role of women and attitudes toward death. In its own way, the financial crisis has been a period of significant upheaval that sparked fundamental change, prompting organizations and companies alike to consider how to do more with fewer resources during a time of economic uncertainty.

"When you have a period of urgency, there are inherent in that period pressures for change and opportunities for change. One of the lessons for me about this time of great urgency that we've been through is what kind of opportunities for important change do we get delivered by that time? How do we take advantage of those opportunities?" she added.

Faust's thirst for learning and her academic discipline as an historian have contributed to her leadership and ability to tackle the most pressing issues at the university. "I think history can give you a tremendous amount of perspective," she observed. "I've learned from history that so much of leadership is helping people deal with change and understand how change happens. History is about the nature of change."

ON A CREST OF A WAVE OF CHANGE

From the beginning, Faust was no stranger to challenging the status quo and trying to effect change. As a child growing up in Virginia in the early 1950s and attending an all-white school and belonging to an all-white church congregation, Faust was troubled by the segregation she saw around her and sought to do something about it. She wrote a letter to a man she thought could make things right: President Dwight Eisenhower. "I am nine years old and I am white but I have many feelings about segregation," she told him.

In an essay published in 2003 in *Harvard Magazine*, Faust reflected on what could have triggered her determination to let the

president know how deeply she felt about the injustice of segregation. "What I remember," she wrote, "is that I heard something on
the radio as I was being driven home from school by Raphael
Johnson—a black man who worked for my family doing everything
from mowing the lawn, shining shoes, and washing floors and
windows to transporting my brothers and me around the county,
entertaining us all the while with quizzes on state and world capitals
or the order of the presidents. I was in the car with Raphael when I
heard something that made me realize that black children did not go
to my school because they were not allowed to, because I was white
and they were not."[2]

What is perhaps most extraordinary about the letter is not just
the fact that Faust wrote it without her parents' knowledge (they
probably would not have encouraged her), but the fact that she
fully expected a reply from President Eisenhower himself. The
perfunctory acknowledgment from the White House was hardly
satisfying for a young girl who wanted change.

"Something hit me as a child that the society I lived in was
unjust. I was just nine years old but I needed to do something
about it," Faust said in our conversation, "I had been taught that
American history was a parade of unfolding justice, and I thought
that was true. I was sent to Sunday school, and I am sure I learned
values there."

Some five decades later, Faust learned that her letter had been
kept and was among the documents in the Eisenhower Library in
Kansas that captured the thoughts of society at the time. As an
historian who often relied on letters, journals, and other primary
sources for research, Faust appreciated being part of history.
Outside of its historic context, Faust's letter also revealed something deeper: her conviction to go against the grain and question
the status quo.

The only daughter in a household with three brothers, Faust
rejected her mother's traditional view of the role of women in society

and her mother's advice that she was living in a man's world and the quicker she accepted that fact, the better it would be for her. For Faust, who was always called by her middle name of Drew instead of her first name of Catharine, that narrow worldview was unacceptable. She became compelled to understand the world around her by exploring its historic roots. In the process, she would achieve more than she ever thought possible.

"It would have been unimaginable for me as a child to think I would end up here, especially when [women at the time] would not have been allowed in the undergraduate library at Harvard," Faust reflected. "I was supposed to get married, have children, and probably not even work." (She is married to Charles Rosenberg, a leading historian of medicine and science and a professor at Harvard; they have two daughters.)

As much of a trailblazer as she has been, Faust readily acknowledged that she has also been the beneficiary of societal change that began to open doors to women of her generation—yet another example of the events that have made her. "I have been on a crest of a wave of change in American society that has opened up possibilities that I could not have expected or envisioned as a child or a young person. And that has been a source of wonder and satisfaction and fulfillment and amazement to me."

Faust contrasted her personal experience of growing up in the early 1950s in a time of limited opportunities for women with the broad array of possibilities for the Harvard students in 2010, male and female, for whom there is also pressure to perform, excel, and succeed. "Students now have so many clear ideas about, 'I must win this prize. I must get this job. I must get into this school. I must have these things.' On the one hand, it probably drives them toward achievement, but it also gives them measures for failure that I never had for myself," she explained. "Yes, I have failed in many things, but I never said I failed because I am not the president of the United States or I don't make X amount of money."

She shared the story of a freshman who told her he wanted to become president of Harvard one day and asked if he could speak with her about how to pursue that goal. Faust told the student she would be happy to meet with him but her advice was not to pin himself down so specifically. "Maybe he will become president of Harvard and maybe he won't. Probably there will be paths that will open for him that will be very fulfilling, and yet he will have it in his mind [that he's going to be Harvard president]. The great statistical likelihood is he will not reach that goal."

Given her own experiences of capitalizing on opportunity and creating change, Faust takes seriously being a role model for the students at Harvard, thus extending the reach of her leadership. Whenever possible, she seizes a moment to tell them that, plans and long-term goals aside, to some degree one's life must unfold. As she observed in her baccalaureate address to the Class of 2008, the key to success and happiness is to pursue what one is most passionate about, take some risks, and see how life turns out. "The answer is you don't know until you try," Faust said in her speech. "But if you don't try to do what you love—whether it is painting or biology or finance—if you don't pursue what you think will be most meaningful, you will regret it. Life is long. There is always time for Plan B. But don't begin with it."[3]

Coming from a history professor who never intended to become a college president, let alone to run Harvard, it is excellent advice. For leaders, too, there needs to be balance between pursuing the long-term plan and handling the opportunities and obstacles that arise in the short term.

LISTEN, LEARN, AND LEAD

Seated in her office with its imposing fireplace and plank floors, Faust was surrounded by the mystique and tradition that is

Harvard, which dates back to the days when Massachusetts was a Puritan colony in the New World. Although she has a deep respect for the traditions at Harvard as a preeminent academy of leadership across all fields of study, she has also been willing to question everything, particularly how the university operates. The time has come, she explained, "to change in order to sustain what matters most."

Before becoming president of Harvard, Faust was an insider at the university, which she joined in 2001 to lead the Radcliffe Institute. She had come to Harvard after twenty-five years on the faculty at the University of Pennsylvania, where she taught history and directed the women's studies programs. Because the Radcliffe Institute did not have any faculty of its own, as the dean Faust had to reach out to faculty across Harvard to get them involved in the institute. That enabled her to get to know people throughout the university beyond the Harvard Faculty of Arts and Sciences, of which she was part as a professor of history. Her ability to seek out others, listen to diverse opinions, and build consensus became leadership strengths and important tools for dealing with crisis and change.

After being named Harvard president, Faust extended her outreach beyond those who knew her as the dean of Radcliffe to every school and department at the university. "My approach to the situation when I took over was just to try to hear from people what was on their minds and to assure constituencies who didn't know me in the university that I cared about what they were doing and that I wanted to know more about it," Faust explained.

Faust's leadership approach was first to listen and learn and then to lead. Listening and learning are essential to building a leader's knowledge and to forging bonds and creating unity around common goals and purpose. For Faust, this meant getting to know every part of the university. Her outreach efforts attracted a stream of people, literally, into her office. Faculty stopped by and sent long letters to discuss what they saw as critical to the future of the university. "People had their eyes on the future and not the past and wanted to discuss how I could help them move to that future in the most effective and collaborative way. That was very helpful," Faust said.

Deep alliances between Faust and the faculty were created through three dean searches undertaken between February and July 2007 in the schools of medicine, arts and sciences, and design. Unlike other institutions where the president essentially approves the recommendations of a search panel, at Harvard the president actually runs the dean search, working closely with an advisory search committee. For Faust, the searches became "forums of outreach" within the university and to alums and leaders in the fields. "These searches were really key for me in defining relationships within three major schools at Harvard and enabling me to speak with a lot of faculty and hear what was on people's minds," she added.

Faust's outreach became even more valuable when she had to face the sudden impact of the financial crisis, which reduced the nearly $37 billion Harvard Endowment by 27 percent by mid-2008 as the market meltdown and a global recession took hold. By mid-2009, the endowment had fallen further to $26 billion, before recouping some of its losses to stand at over $27 billion by mid-2010. For Harvard, which depended on its endowment for 38 percent of its operating budget, it was time for dramatic action.

LEADERSHIP AND COMMUNICATION

How a leader communicates during a crisis directly affects people's perceptions of the severity of the problem, their confidence in the leader's ability to find the way forward, and their assessment of how the organization is equipped to respond. For Faust, responding to the crisis meant getting a handle on its effect on the university portfolio and communicating quickly to the Harvard community. In a marked departure from past practice, Harvard issued a public statement about its anticipated losses even before the fiscal year had ended. "I needed the community to understand how serious this was," Faust explained. "People had always thought, 'Oh, our endowment is so well managed, nothing will ever happen to it.' This was a different moment. We had to get ready and adjust."

Because Faust did not have in-depth financial expertise, she sought out the advice of some of the best minds in the field who were at the university. "Harvard is filled with talented people," she noted. Thanks to her seat on the Harvard Management Company board, she received a crash course in Harvard's investments, which helped her speak credibly to the challenges. Comfortable in her own skin, Faust was able to ask questions in order to get up to speed on the scope of the problem and the kinds of solutions that were needed, becoming a confident leader during the crisis. "I wouldn't say that you would want to use me as your financial advisor, it hasn't gotten to that," she quipped. "But I did get a pretty good sense of what needed to be done and how to think about the problems we faced."

Putting herself on the front lines of communication, Faust went out to the various schools at Harvard to explain to the deans and faculty about the severity of the problem. "I thought it was very important that I talk about the finances and not just bring in a financial person. They needed to know that I understood the problem . . . that I got it and I was dealing with it," she recalled.

Her firsthand experience in the midst of the crisis confirmed what Faust had always believed to be true: that leadership and communication are closely tied. "In a time of crisis what people want from their leaders is to understand what on earth is going on," she added. "It's the leader who has to help individuals understand by defining the situation and the path through it. And that's what I tried to do."

Her response to the crisis also revealed her leadership style: collaborative and with a preference for addressing issues early on. "I like to be ahead of things," she observed. "I'm not a procrastinator because that just means I am going to suffer through it longer: first, to worry it to death, and then I'm going to have to deal with it anyway. I would much rather try to figure out what's the right path and take it early on. I would prefer to have some [influence over] a problem rather than be a victim of the problem."

Her words call to mind the old saying that, as a leader, you can choose to avoid reality, but you cannot avoid the consequences of avoiding reality. Clearly, Faust was dealing with a particularly harsh reality of a global financial and economic crisis.

Harvard's response encompassed both the immediate steps of reducing expenses and budgets and longer-term strategies such as exploring how different disciplines could collaborate in new ways. To illustrate the point, Faust recalled a visit she made to the Harvard Stem Cell Institute where she was shown images of cells to which certain compounds had been added to test whether the cells were protected from being infected with amyotrophic lateral sclerosis (ALS), or Lou Gehrig's disease. Intrigued by the imaging, Faust asked a researcher whether the idea had originated from physics or biology. His reply was very telling of the state of cutting-edge research. "He said all the fields are merging," Faust said excitedly. "Life sciences and physical sciences are breaking down the distinctions."

She sees the same merging of disciplines between social science and humanities as well as social science and natural sciences.

Interdependence allows multiple disciplines to tackle major issues, such as healthcare delivery in the United States, which involves Harvard's schools of business, public health, and medicine, as well as the sociology and economics faculty. These developments speak to the essence of Faust's mission of determining "how we, as an institution that has so many strengths, really take advantage of our knowledge."

The answer to that question could result in increased collaboration at Harvard to further research and thought leadership at the university. As distinctions between academic disciplines blur, there could be more opportunities for faculty in one school to teach in another, thus making better use of resources while sharing valuable knowledge.

THE MAKING OF FUTURE LEADERS

Responding to the financial crisis has also allowed Faust to tackle issues that are more philosophical in nature, such as examining the link between higher education and economic growth, and if a better educated workforce can help propel the economy forward. To focus on that point alone, Faust advised, would be to neglect a larger question about the value of humanities as well as what she called the more theoretical aspects of higher education. "Not just to train people but to educate them for a life," she added. "Not just a vocational capacity but rather an ability to be someone who can ask the big, difficult questions. I think all of these issues have been put on the table by the financial crisis. We, as a leading institution in the field of higher education, need to pose those questions and come up with some answers."

Faust thinks deeply about the role of Harvard in making future leaders who need to understand the intersection of leadership and responsibility—who need not only to lead others, but also to think beyond their own self-interests. "It means your career is not just about enhancing your own talents or your own resources and building a good life for yourself," she explained. "Leadership means having a sense of responsibility and a sense of ethical commitment to society and to those you are leading."

When we met, it was still too soon to comment on Faust's legacy to the institution. Nonetheless, she did reflect on the difference she hopes to make during her years as president. Top of her list is the issue of access, making sure that people feel as if they are part of the Harvard community regardless of race, gender, or economic circumstances. She described her vision of Harvard as a "porous institution that really draws talent and enhances and welcomes that talent—a vibrant intellectual community. That is how we serve our own goals by getting the best talent, and it's also how we serve the world best, as we serve the people who can take advantage of what we have to offer."

Second on her list was the hope that when her term is done she can look back on these times and say she took advantage of the opportunity that events presented to institute important and lasting change. "I hope I will be able to say that I took this moment when change was possible and I used it to improve Harvard in a variety of dimensions, some of them organizational and administrative, but more important the kinds of intellectual connections that our interdependence [between schools and disciplines] can foster," she observed.

As Faust responds to external catalysts and creates some of her own, there is no doubt that she is leading Harvard into and through a period of questioning and discernment. This prompted Faust to offer one last item on her legacy wish list: "that we really asked hard questions and made ourselves better and that we decided that just because we've done some things one way doesn't mean that we wouldn't change it."

Faust faced a crisis without flinching and then chose to look for the opportunity in the midst of turmoil and uncertainty. She shares that attitude with many great leaders who always view the other side of crisis as opportunity because change is inevitable. As a lifelong learner and a student of history, Faust has demonstrated the importance of drawing parallels between past and present and using the lessons learned to chart a course to a more solid future.

To me, the most important leadership word is courage *because as a leader you have to be at ease with the possibility that you might fail.*

—Olli-Pekka Kallasvuo, former CEO
and president, Nokia Corporation;
chairman, Nokia Siemens Networks

Chapter Eleven

OLLI-PEKKA KALLASVUO: COURAGE

When I first sat down in March 2010 to talk with Olli-Pekka Kallasvuo, who was then CEO and president of Nokia, he made a comment that in many ways shaped this book: "To me, the most important leadership word is *courage* because as a leader you have to be at ease with the possibility that you might fail." From his statement, as well as the observations of other leaders interviewed, the seeds for this book were sown.

Later in 2010, Kallasvuo, who goes by his initials "OPK," had to live through stinging criticism on a global stage. Despite a 34-percent global market share for its cell phones, Nokia found itself the subject of speculation by bloggers and analysts about its ability to compete, particularly in the smartphone arena. This perception led to the view that Nokia needed a change at the top. In September 2010, OPK stepped down as CEO and president of Nokia, although he continues as the chairman of its Nokia Siemens Networks venture. Given all of what he experienced, his perspective on courage and facing failure became even more important to capture in this book.

In our follow-up conversation in October 2010, OPK neither assigned blame nor intimated that the change in management was unwarranted or unfair. In fact, he rarely spoke about himself; rather, his comments were mostly about the company he clearly identified with and to which he remains exceedingly loyal. "It's not about whether it's fair, or right or wrong, but what is best for the organization," OPK added.

During his long career at the Espoo, Finland–based telecommunications giant, OPK accomplished much. He joined Nokia in 1980 as a general counsel and rose through the ranks. A member of the company's executive board starting in 1990, OPK became chief financial officer in 1992 and then, in 2006, president and chief executive officer. During that time Nokia transformed itself into a mobile telephone powerhouse and became a recognizable international brand.

Yet there is no denying that OPK exited company leadership in a way that was not exactly as he would have planned. For all CEOs, there will come a time when, whether by choice or not, a leader's term comes to an end and someone else will take over. "The possibility is there, if not every day then every week or month, in a CEO's position. And we all know that," OPK observed. "It will come to an end, sooner or later, and in different ways. You have to be at ease with that."

When we spoke the second time, OPK had already transitioned out of the CEO role at Nokia, turning over the reins to Stephen Elop, who had headed Microsoft's Business Division. In announcing the executive change, Nokia called it "the right time to accelerate the company's renewal; to bring in new executive leadership with different skills and strengths in order to drive company success."[1]

With grace and class, OPK echoed those same themes in his comments about stepping down from management at Nokia. "Renewal needs to take place, and sometimes on the top level. It's about the things that need to happen and what the organization needs. At the end of the day, it's the board of directors that is responsible for those calls. They need to make them," he said.

In the telecommunications industry, the pace of change is relentless, and the process of implementing it is fluid and ongoing.

OPK clearly grasped the dynamic environment in which he was immersed, saying, "Everything changes so rapidly. There is major challenge and major opportunity, as well."

Among the challenges for Nokia was its portfolio of smartphones. Its long-awaited Nokia N8, the first of its smartphones with a new software platform, began shipping in late September 2010. In a statement issued in July 2010, OPK had promised that the new smartphones would "kick-start Nokia's fight back at the higher end of the market."[2]

Such a challenge was daunting given the crowded telecommunications marketplace and the lingering aftermath of the worst recession since the Great Depression and a global economic slowdown. No doubt the management change at Nokia reflected this reality. "It comes down to whether you are seen as making progress or not. It's a question of credibility and confidence," OPK observed. "And sometimes I feel the situation can get so difficult and so time consuming that no matter what you do, there is some realignment that needs to happen."

Tellingly, OPK did not defend his record or second-guess decisions he had made in the past by speculating on what, if anything, he would change. "Mistakes are made; mistakes are not made. Everybody makes mistakes, but at the end of the day, the lesson is you do your best. You do your best to make the best decisions you can," he observed. "Sometimes they lead to an outcome that you want and sometimes not. But knowing what I did know and with the insight I had at the time, I would have made the same calls."

In today's highly competitive and fast-paced business environment, leaders need to make the best decisions they can based on the information at hand, which may be incomplete or subject to change. A leader won't always be right; no one ever is. Some decisions will prove to have been prudent and advantageous and others will fall short of the mark. Whatever the outcome, the leader needs to live with his or her decisions.

PASSION AND EXCITEMENT

As CEO of Nokia, OPK may have lacked the instant recognition of the heavyweights in the technology field. What he did have, however, was passion for the mission. During our first conversation, I noticed that the more OPK talked about the company, the more visibly energized he became. "I am testing myself almost on a weekly basis: Am I excited? Is everything we are doing exciting on a personal level? From that excitement you get the energy. If you lose your ability to get excited, people will notice," OPK said.

Even after stepping down as CEO, OPK exhibited that same passion. "I am really willing to do things for the company from the sidelines," he said. "I love the company and I love the people. I will root for them."

As for his successor, OPK said he had already known Elop from the industry. When the two men spoke as part of the management transition, OPK said he "committed to give every possible support I can give going forward."

Although his role as chairman of Nokia Siemens Networks, a telecommunications services venture of Nokia and Siemens, is a nonexecutive position, OPK expressed gratitude for the opportunity to continue contributing to Nokia. "It's an important part of the company," he said of Nokia Siemens. "The fact that I can continue to serve the company in another capacity is a great example of how things can happen and move forward. It's the best illustration of the fact that people can be mature and continue to cooperate and they can continue to work together in another part [of the organization]. I think that [this] is also an example of trust."

In every person's life and career, there are momentary failures, both personal and professional. Beyond specific episodes, however, failure is harder to measure and quantify. "Failure is a difficult concept because it is not black and white, although it might come down to a black-and-white situation," OPK said. In other words, a person can fail in the moment and suffer a setback but not be a failure.

Leadership, like life, is not a "winner takes all" proposition that hinges entirely on the last conquest. Across one's career is a spectrum of events, both positive and negative, that build resilience, impart confidence, and develop wisdom, allowing a leader to contribute from the sum of those experiences.

Instilling Confidence Through Constant Progress

As CEO of Nokia, OPK's task was a considerable one: leading Nokia through a significant transformation from the world's largest manufacturer of mobile phone handsets into a company that also provides consumers with access to applications, or "apps" as they are known. For Nokia, the transition meant "new skills, new capabilities, new partners, and new people," as OPK explained at the time.

As a company, Nokia has had a long heritage of metamorphosis. Over the course of a century and a half, the company we now know as Nokia has been involved in businesses such as pulp and paper, rubber, cable manufacturing, and cellular telephones. Its transformation from one major industry to another painted a picture of industrial evolution, from heavy industry to high tech. Although its latest transformation into a producer of software apps put Nokia into a crowded marketplace with big-name competitors such as Apple, Nokia had no choice but to move forward.

In the midst of such change, OPK saw it was his responsibility to instill confidence in those he led. As he observed, when uncertainty or challenge arises, people will look to the leader to see if he or she is confident and energized. "You have to win them over, one by one: twenty-five today, two hundred tomorrow. That does not happen overnight. It takes years sometimes, from the time the first guy comes on board until the last guy—and sometimes the last guy will not," OPK commented.

Creating cohesion and generating excitement among employees take more than a vision; tangible progress and achievements are paramount. "They need victories," OPK said. "They want the possibility to celebrate. Vision alone is not enough anymore. . . . Constant progress is needed."

During his leadership at Nokia, a global company with 65,000 employees worldwide (125,000 including Nokia Siemens) comprising ninety-five different nationalities, OPK made communication and outreach a top priority. He was always aware of the power and reach of his words. Whether he was speaking at an industry event or talking to employees, virtually everything he said was rapidly disseminated through blogs that report on the company's every move.

The greater the challenge, OPK knew, the more communication was needed—constant and as close to real time as possible. "There is no shortcut here," he commented. "You must communicate: 'This is what we have this month, and this is where we have made progress. This is where we have not made progress.'"

OPK gave the example of when Nokia set a target of eighty million users of its apps and services by the end of 2009. Rather than keep that information confidential and privy only to top management, OPK announced the target broadly. Furthermore, everyone in the company was to be kept abreast of incremental progress on a weekly basis. In Nokia's head office in Finland, monitors were installed to give employees updates at a glance. "I was really nervous about that because I knew this could backfire," OPK recalled.

In the end, Nokia made the goal, but that was not why OPK shared this anecdote. He meant it as an example of the level of exposure and disclosure that was expected of him as he steered Nokia through execution of its strategy.

"The granularity of information that people want and need is so much more. When I was a younger man, people within the company knew when 'this is something I should not talk about with everybody.' Nowadays, in this blogging and communication culture, everything is discussed openly," he said.

In the closely watched and highly anticipated technology sector, the degree of transparency required is incredible and far more than in the past. This clearly introduces an element of risk for the leader: failures are made just as public as victories. "If a product is late, it's not just the people in R&D who know. People start blogging about it," OPK said.

As the CEO and the public face of Nokia, whatever happened or didn't happen on OPK's watch was ultimately his responsibility.

OPENNESS AND TRANSPARENCY

Although OPK described himself as a private person by nature, he embraced the openness and transparency that were required of him as CEO. He credited what he recalled as one of the best pieces of advice he had been given. He was a few months into his job as the CFO nearly twenty years ago when someone older and more experienced called him aside and explained, "It's very important for you to remember that although you are still an individual, you are not only a person, you are also a representative of a system or a corporation. As a leader in an important position, you have to step up."

OPK realized that he could no longer divide himself between a private persona and a public one. Nothing was private anymore, a sentiment that has been shared by many other leaders in this book. "I had a role and a responsibility as a senior leader to lead people, to set an example. I really took that to heart. For me, personally, that was good advice," he said.

His willingness to be open won OPK many admirers among employees and followers of the company. Comfortable with himself, OPK found that off-the-cuff remarks came naturally, along with his warm, self-deprecating humor. For example, when he heard the title of this book, OPK quipped, "That is certainly applicable here," and laughed.

Even after stepping down as Nokia's CEO, OPK's mind-set toward being in the public eye had not changed. He endured the glare of attention in numerous media and blog reports through the management transition. Although he was no longer the CEO, OPK was still a high-profile leader and needed to show grace under fire for the good of the company. At the same time, OPK received an outpouring of support, including from employees. As we talked it was clear that he greatly appreciated this affirmation of his efforts to forge bonds across the company. "As I look back, I feel that I can hold my head high," he said. "With that [positive employee] feedback, I have been pretty much at ease with the situation."

When we first spoke, OPK talked about how much he enjoyed leading people and was comfortable with the exposure that comes with being the head of a nearly $60 billion global company. Yet, looking back on his long career, he admitted that he did not always consider himself to be a natural leader; rather, he grew into the role. Even as a general counsel he had found himself drawn to the business side of things and preferred helping people find solutions rather than telling them what they could or could not do. After moving into finance, he became a CFO who operated "more as a strategy person than as an accountant."

OPK brought his passion for business strategy to the top executive position at Nokia. He understood that intelligence must be gathered outside the company in order to be in step with the consumer as much as possible. In urban areas, Nokia studies con-sumers to find out what matters most to them. In developing markets, where there is great potential for mobile communication to make positive changes, Nokia dispatches teams of anthropologists. "We are providing the connection," OPK said, "but it is the [consumer's] choice to say what is important."

Gathering business intelligence on the outside is a significant change from years past. To illustrate the point, OPK engaged in a brief history lesson, starting with the 1930s and 1940s when business intelligence was on the inside and often housed in manufacturing. By the 1950s, sales and marketing became more valued in order to reach consumers. Later, shareholder value was made a priority, which put an emphasis on the finance department. Today, companies seek intelligence across the marketplace to determine what consumers want now and what they are likely to ask for tomorrow.

"How do you sense what is happening and then productize based on that sense? The intelligence is not inside, it is outside," OPK observed. "So how do you sense what is happening now, especially on a global level?"

THE EVOLVING CULTURE

As CEO, OPK was also instrumental in the ongoing evolution of the Nokia culture. Over the span of his thirty years at the company—longer than any other executive—he had seen many changes. The company's cultural foundation was still largely intact, although elements of it had evolved. Continuity, as he saw it, was essential. "In India, there is a saying: if you have a knife that is old and the blade and handle have been changed several times but never at the same time, it is still the same knife. There is something like that in an organization—something that is more than the people who are working there at the same time. In this case, in spite of the fact that the people are not the same, there is a lot of similarity in the culture."

OPK believed culture was expressed in the values of the company. To be most effective, values cannot cascade down from upper management. Rather, they must be embraced, even to the point of being defined, at the grassroots level and then spread throughout the organization. He described an involved process at Nokia in 2008 to assess its corporate values, starting with discussions held among employees in different parts of the world. After local groups gathered, representatives were then chosen to attend regional meetings where discussions continued. A final meeting of about forty-five people was held in Helsinki for two days. On the afternoon of the second day, OPK, who was CEO at the time, joined the session.

"I went there to that meeting as if to approve or disapprove, but when I got there, I could sense the passion and the energy and the commitment as they were explaining how they had reached that point and what it meant," he recalled. "I realized that I didn't even have the option of saying, 'No, this is not correct.' The employees had come up with the values and what they meant. I realized that I could not call this off. This was it, whether I liked it or not."

The final step was a seventy-two-hour continuous Internet-based discussion involving ten thousand people in the company, including management. "It was not only the outcome, but the process, that made people buy into that—as opposed to trying to cascade down [the values]," OPK commented. "You really cannot order change in culture."

THE IMPORTANCE OF COURAGE

Given all the changes swirling around him as CEO, it was no wonder that OPK chose courage as the most important leadership concept. During his leadership, there was a lot riding on his shoulders. On the one hand, he called decision making "a team sport," involving senior managers and drawing from information across the company. "It's so big and complex that if I started to make decisions by shooting from the hip, I would make a lot of mistakes," he said at the time. On the other hand, there were occasions when OPK had to step up and make a decision, which required courage.

"Sometimes there are those moments when you simply have to say, 'This is what we will do.' And it's also what people want to hear," OPK explained. "It's quite interesting that very often people will say, 'Oh, it's difficult,' but when someone else says, 'This is what we are going to do,' there is great relief. A difficult matter has been decided."

Although he has much to be proud of in terms of his long career at Nokia, OPK did acknowledge some sadness over the management transition. But the feeling of loss was fleeting. With courage came the clarity and acceptance of change, even though it was initiated by others.

"Things need to happen, and renewal is sometimes necessary," OPK added. "I don't have an intellectual problem with that."

Since his departure as CEO, OPK has moved on, setting his sights firmly on the future both for himself and for Nokia. He has internalized the lessons learned in the midst of a transition that may have been unplanned, but in reality was not unexpected when it finally happened. "One always needs to look forward," OPK said, an encouraging reminder for all leaders that out of setbacks new opportunities can spring.

What you have to do for employees is to be truthful and give them the facts, but you are also obligated to leave them with a sense of belief that the problems can be overcome and solved.

—Anne Mulcahy, retired chairman
and former CEO, Xerox

Chapter Twelve

ANNE MULCAHY: RESILIENCE

Anne Mulcahy began our conversation with a deep breath and a hearty laugh. "It's an interesting time," she said, clearly bemused by her own understatement. In was early May 2010, and she was retiring as chairman after nearly a decade in leadership and thirty-four years as a company employee. As we talked, Mulcahy turned thoughtful for a moment, obviously wrestling with the fact that although she knew it was the right time to leave, in her heart she was having difficulty with the transition to life after Xerox.

"If you had told me in 2000 that I could have walked out on my own two feet with a company that was in good shape with a great successor, I would have said, 'Yahoo! The sooner the better.' And then you get here and it's very hard to let go. So there is part of me that is struggling to let go and not have this thing be part of my life that has defined my life for so long," she admitted.

As Mulcahy spoke, I could not help but compare her with the star athlete who knows it's best to retire at the top of her game, better not to stay too long, and yet still doesn't want to stop playing. Her reticence was understandable, given all she had been through with the company where she started out as a sales representative in 1976 following two years in banking. She joined Xerox largely because she needed a job but also because she enjoyed the competition she found in sales, which offered a level playing field of results-based compensation that was particularly important for women at the time.

She honed her resilience in sales, where most of the time the answer was no until, at last, there was a yes. Her ability to endure the temporary disappointments in order to savor the final victory became an invaluable skill as she moved up in the company, with senior positions in sales, human resources, and marketing, and later in corporate management.

Mulcahy's reluctance to leave also reflected the fact that she had accomplished the near-impossible at Xerox after she took the reins in August 2001, a time when the company was in turmoil and not expected to survive. Her appointment followed a failed succession a year earlier, when one CEO was fired because of a lack of confidence in his ability to solve deeply entrenched problems, and the predecessor CEO, who had remained chairman, had to step back in temporarily to run the company. During the shuffling of players in the top spot, Mulcahy was promoted to president and chief operating officer, but that was hardly an adequate grooming for a CEO, which usually takes place over several years with strategic assignments in various executive and operating posts.

After becoming CEO, a job she had never particularly wanted or sought over the years, Mulcahy immediately had to address declining sales, increasing competition, huge debt, and questionable past accounting practices that sparked a Securities and Exchange Commission (SEC) investigation, all of which formed what she has called a "perfect storm" of problems. For Xerox, after losing almost $300 million in 2000 and under the enormous weight of nearly $19 billion in debt, bankruptcy seemed inevitable.

Undeterred, the straight-talking Mulcahy set about to tackle monumental tasks with whatever resources she could muster. Always resilient, she wasn't about to give up but she wasn't going to kid herself, either. Even she thought at times that the company would probably go under. With a glimmer of hope, she came up with a plan and recruited others to support it, starting with the most valuable members on the team: the employees.

"I told employees the truth, the brutal facts. I always went through what the challenges were, how much debt we had. What you have to do for employees is to be truthful and give them the facts, but you are also obligated to leave them with a sense of belief that the problems can be overcome and solved," Mulcahy recalled. "I had that sense of belief. But I also had to be realistic enough to know that the odds were set up against us."

One of Xerox's problems stemmed from that fact that it had fully drawn on a $7 billion revolving line of credit from no fewer than fifty-eight banks. In order to renew that credit line, which was essential to keeping Xerox in business, all fifty-eight banks had to agree to sign off. After hoarding about $3 billion in cash to pay down a small portion of the debt, Mulcahy set about getting the necessary signatures, convincing them that extending credit to Xerox wasn't money down the drain. "There were probably fifty-eight banks that thought we were going bankrupt and this thing was going to be a loss," she explained. "We had to literally go out and get every single one to agree. We really got down to the wire. There were two banks that held out on us." When the banks finally signed, Xerox received a reprieve. Mulcahy had bet on there being a silver lining amidst all the dark clouds shrouding the company, and she was right.

"There wasn't a moment that wasn't intensely focused on making sure the place survived," she said. "It really wasn't that hard to stay focused and to some degree be optimistic because the stakes were so high. You just had to believe, especially when you were looking, at the time, at eighty thousand people who were dependent on the company. You better find that silver lining to hang onto because that's what it's all about."

For Mulcahy, saving Xerox was personal. By the time she became CEO, the company had been her corporate home and the center of her professional identity for more than two decades. No matter how much she identified with the company, however, Mulcahy could not take on the CEO role without creating some separation between herself and the company's fate. As she put it, "I had to take the job with a sense that I would do everything I could; I would do my very best. But I couldn't let it destroy me if I was unsuccessful. There has to be some separation so that you are able to live with yourself."

Undaunted by the potential that the turnaround of Xerox would fail, Mulcahy was able to face the enormity of the task that lay ahead of her. Because she saw the risks so clearly, she was able to put together a plan. She sought to adapt corporate culture, keeping what was good and jettisoning what was bad. Central to that was creating a sense of common purpose around rescuing Xerox, a mission that brought the entire team together.

As CEO, Mulcahy proved capable of making the tough decisions: cutting $1 billion in expenses and laying off nearly one-third of the workforce. Some of the choices were especially painful, such as shutting down a business that Mulcahy had helped to establish. Bad news, she insisted, had to be delivered in person and communicated in such a way that the people affected understood that actions were being taken to save the company and, wherever possible, to spare jobs.

Mulcahy recalled the experience in advice she gave recently to a friend who needed to sell his business. "First of all deliver the message in person. It's a tough decision, but I think that if you are there people will understand that you are taking on that very difficult message. That helps. Also it's not about them. Separate the people from the business consequences so that they don't feel a sense of personal failure," she recounted. "You're going to do everything possible to help them land on their feet in whatever context that is so that their interests are protected as you go through this process. That's it. There is not a lot more you can say. You can't avoid the decision of doing what's right for the business. You have to communicate it in a way that people understand why you are making the decision and protect as much of their sense of pride as possible."

Setting Priorities

In the midst of the turnaround, the success of which was hardly ensured, Mulcahy struggled with mounting problems and never-ending demands. "The banks pretty much owned the company. The analysts were killing us, and the media were killing us. We were trying to tell our story and keep afloat," she remembered. Into that swirl of chaos stepped the voice of reason in the person of Warren Buffett, whose advice Mulcahy had sought. "He basically simplified the whole thing: 'Stop. There is only one way you are going to get results, and that's by keeping your customers loyal and your people engaged and motivated. Get everything else out of the way,'" Mulcahy remembered. "It was like a cleansing breath—whoa! That's it. That's what I had to do. It kept a lot of noise out of the system for me and allowed me to focus with a lot more clarity than I had."

As CEOs well know, with so many people vying for their time and attention, prioritizing can be easier said than done. But just like the captain of the team must focus first on the players, a leader's priority must be the people on whom he or she relies to carry out the strategy and produce results in the field. Asked what advice she would give to new CEOs, Mulcahy drew on this lesson learned in the midst of the battle: stay focused on the most important constituencies, as Mulcahy called them, "your people and your customers."

"As a CEO, there is so much to worry about, so many constituencies. Focusing on customers and employees always has to be the place you measure your impact on the job. That guidance actually has made me constantly look at my calendar and move out the stuff that's peripheral and make sure that the vast majority of my time is spent on the two sets of people who actually make the place tick. It's not analysts, it's not shareholders, it's not bankers, it's not industry people, it's not competitors. It is actually your customers and your employees. They keep you market connected," Mulcahy observed. "If you really are engaged in connecting with your employees you discover problems and opportunities early enough to do something about them. It's a powerful focus. Although it makes all the sense in the world, it's really hard to do unless you approach it in a very conscious way."

Being resolved to stay connected with what is most important, however, often proves difficult to achieve. CEOs face a host of things that divert their attention and consume their time. For a new CEO, the pull to go in a million different directions is particularly strong.

"Business councils, business roundtables, people who want you to serve on their boards. . . . You've got a million things that are stretching you in different directions," she added. "Just stay focused on the fact that if you can't spend the vast majority of your time on your customers and your employees, then you've lost your way in terms of developing priorities."

THE IMPORTANCE OF FOLLOWERSHIP

As Mulcahy knew well, none of her bold plans to resuscitate and transform Xerox would be possible if others did not sign on to the plan. She needed to inspire followership, which she described as influencing and aligning people around a common set of goals and unifying teams to carry out the mission of the organization. Followership cannot be forced or mandated; it is not the product of a communications plan. Followership occurs on the human level, with authenticity and trust. In Mulcahy's case, standing for honesty and integrity was critical as Xerox struggled with a loss of credibility.

"I think whether you call it honesty or integrity or authenticity, I do think that people see that clearly right from the start. They know it when they see it, and they know it when they don't see it. And they respond accordingly. I think you have to build that level of trust that allows people to place responsibility with you, which is very important," she added.

During the worst of it, one of the hardest things to face at the company, where it was not unusual for people to retire after fifty years, was the shame and embarrassment that employees felt. "I have to say, one of the most painful experiences for the people was the time they had to hang their heads and say they worked for Xerox," Mulcahy recalled. "As we looked at that and asked, 'What do we want to accomplish here?' yes, we wanted to get out of debt and make money. But I think the overriding goal was to be proud of the company. The way I articulated that at the time was that I wanted people to feel so good about Xerox that they would want their kids or their grand-children to work at this company."

Mulcahy worked to regain employees' trust, assuring them that the problems of the past would not be repeated or tolerated in the future. As a leader, she had to let employees know what they could expect in terms of values and behavior. To establish an emotional link that allowed followership to grow, Mulcahy had to become transparent, willing to let people know who she was and what she stood for. At the same time, she could not do all the talking. As she traveled from place to place meeting with Xerox employees, hers was high-touch leadership at its best and most demanding.

"Even in a world where it's easy to communicate in lots of ways, I don't think anything replaces touch. You have to get out there. If you are running a big global company, you actually have to go to them, and I think you've got to do it frequently. Your messages have to be consistent and relatively simple," Mulcahy observed. "The challenge is being able to deliver the message in a way that is relevant to a whole spectrum of people across a company. I don't think it comes from PowerPoint slides. I actually think you have to tell stories that people can relate to and see themselves in and feel a sense of belonging to the organization. They understand what we are doing, and they understand how they can contribute. They feel that there is a sense of fairness about the fact that they can participate."

In order to deliver the message, Mulcahy advised, leaders have to "log the miles"—meaning traveling to meet with employees in person. Otherwise, the dynamic, particularly with difficult or challenging issues, is not a dialogue, but a directive that comes from the top. "It's not talking to, but talking with, that allows this kind of communication to take place. It can be reinforced by great technology and tools and communication vehicles, but I don't think people can get the sense of the leadership dynamic of the company without the ability to touch and see and interact on a personal basis," she added.

Turning a No to a Yes

Although Mulcahy was not groomed to become CEO, she was not without experiences that equipped her for the job. For one, she had spent several years in human resources, which admittedly is not a typical training ground for becoming CEO. Yet Mulcahy described it as an invaluable experience that taught her to "look at the business through the lens of the people . . . getting the talent, retaining the talent, and keeping the talent engaged."

"We think of HR as a function and a technical set of competencies versus the strategic importance of the asset of the people whom you manage in the company. Great leaders happen to be great HR managers, even though they may not have spent a day in the technical side of HR," she added. "I think we have to do a better job of thinking about HR in a deeper and more strategic way."

Perhaps her best training, however, came from her fifteen years in sales, which made her nearly impervious to being discouraged by failure in pursuit of success. "Every day is a win-lose proposition in sales, and losses are the ways you actually adapt and learn and do it better the next time," Mulcahy said. "Every single no is an opportunity to reflect and ask, 'How do you get to a yes?'"

As a leader, Mulcahy relied on the capacity she developed in sales to listen to customers and to understand what determines the difference between those who lose and those who adapt and win. Being flexible and tenacious became even more important when handling larger clients and strategically important deals involving senior leadership. This point was brought home when Xerox lost a huge account with a major bank after having had the business for ten years. "It was very painful. It was a time when we could not afford to lose a buck, and we lost this deal. We had it for a decade, and we ended up getting thrown out for our competition," Mulcahy remembered.

The first priority was to rally the team, to help them see that even after a setback, such as losing a major customer, future success was possible. "I remember meeting with the Xerox team and saying, 'Hey, we have got to turn this around. We had their business for a really long time. So first you have to say thank you for the business, and then we have to listen and understand what went wrong— because it went wrong.'"

Under Mulcahy's direction, attention shifted quickly from the loss to learning the lessons and putting a plan together to win back the business. Mulcahy led the charge by writing a letter to the bank CEO. "I basically said I want to thank you for the decade of business that we were privileged to earn but we blew it. We didn't meet your expectations. We're going to begin to listen and learn, even though we don't have your business today, and work toward getting your business back."

The letter was so well received, the bank CEO sent a copy to all of his sales people, saying, "I've been searching for how we're supposed to lose, and this is it. This is how you are supposed to lose," Mulcahy recalled. It took a few years, but Xerox did, indeed, win back the bank's business. In the process, Mulcahy taught her team a valuable lesson. "It was turning a failure into something that created a path for winning," she explained. "That is really important. You take a deep breath and get over it and get back on the horse and make sure you win."

Mulcahy showcased the approach of turning setbacks into opportunities to learn, describing herself as "a better learner from pain than I am from success." As she said, "I'm in the category of you can read six pages about yourself and you'll remember the one line that said something negative."

Through hard work and tenacity, Mulcahy's plan worked. By 2006, Xerox made more than $1 billion. Its comeback, however, was more than just shoring up its financials. The company also reshaped its business strategy, improved competitiveness, invested in R&D, and offered new products and services. This was far more than just a turnaround, which connotes a short-term focus. It was the execution of a long-term plan. "We define turnaround as someone coming into a company and painting the walls and cleaning it up for disposition in two or three years. That was clearly not what we had done. Did we turn around Xerox? Yes. I would also like to think that we transformed Xerox in the process. Turnaround does not give justice to the fact that we put Xerox in a position to be successful over the long term," she explained.

What was also interesting to observe was how Mulcahy never let the possibility of failing keep her from taking appropriate risks. She knew that no matter how conservative a company is, without some level of risk taking it will cease to grow. "Taking risks is something that a leader has to do in order to really perform and keep the company moving forward in a direction. I worry about that because I think we sometimes equate risk with only the downside versus the upside," she observed. "I think the upside risks are the ones that good leaders have to be willing to jump into, to take and fail occasionally, but to make those kinds of decisions."

Even with her tenure rapidly coming to a close, Mulcahy was still processing some of the lessons learned from Xerox and voiced a few regrets. She candidly reflected on steps she would have rather not taken, such as the sale of Xerox's Chinese and Hong Kong operations, including 50 percent of its Fuji Xerox joint venture, which left the company with only a 25-percent stake. "That was not something I wanted to do," Mulcahy admitted. "But that $1.6 billion [received from the deals] was a lifeline. I didn't have a lot of choices other than to do something to give us permission to live another day. So do I call that a regret, yeah. But would I do it differently? I don't think so because I did the best with what I had at that point in time."

LEARNING TO SAY GOOD-BYE

Even after all she had been through at the helm of Xerox, at the very end of her career Mulcahy faced one of the biggest challenges of all: leaving. "You don't get to do this job with your heart and your head and everything you've got to give without it becoming a big portion of who you are," she said.

Her personal feelings aside, Mulcahy had committed to a succession process to turn over management of the company to Ursula Burns, a thirty-year Xerox employee who was identified years ago as the most likely successor and groomed for the top job. It was the board's decision, Mulcahy explained, to have a "gracious transition," even though from her own perspective it would have been easier to go out all at once, retiring as chairman and CEO. Instead, in July 2009 Mulcahy stepped down as CEO and turned the day-to-day running of the company over to Burns, while remaining chairman for ten more months.

"I got advice from several people who said, 'Do not do this!' But the succession process is more about others than it is about you. Ursula was ready for the job, and I was ready to leave—probably. It's much easier for your people, your customers, and your shareholders to see this gradual transition. At the end of the day, instead of it being a dramatic departure, it's kind of ho-hum," Mulcahy shared.

The fact that Mulcahy took over in the midst of chaos also colored the choices that were made for her departure. The board did not want a repeat performance, and neither did Mulcahy. A successful transition after her long reign was paramount. "The reality is the company probably benefits from that transitional process where you get a fresh set of thinking and ideas to mix it up a bit," she added.

Mulcahy's honesty about the process is enlightening for other leaders who will face their own succession issues. At times succession can seem like little more than an intellectual exercise to check off the boxes of what has been done. Mulcahy showed the importance and intensity of process, which is not about the leaders, even though they are personally and emotionally involved, but about the health, stability, and longevity of the organization.

"Succession has got to be like any other business objective: set some expectations and set some activities. Make it work and make it happen," Mulcahy advised. "If this were all about me, I probably wouldn't be leaving when I am. But this is all about what's right for Xerox, and that's why the process really has to be done well."

In order to make it work, Mulcahy and Burns came up with their own plan to make the transition less painful and awkward for both of them. "I said, 'Here's the guidebook, okay? It's one sentence so here it is: I've got to be smart, and you've got to be gracious. I've got to be smart enough to get myself out of the way, and you've got to be gracious enough when I get myself in the middle to be a little bit respectful.'" Throughout the transition period, the code words *gracious* and *smart* helped the two leaders stay off each other's toes even when they strayed onto each other's turf.

Although there was a smile on Mulcahy's face as we spoke, the emotion in her voice was clear. It broadcast through her well-chosen and thoughtful words a simple message: leaving is tough. Clearly that was the reason why, on the day of our meeting with only a couple of weeks to go before her official retirement, Mulcahy had yet to fill the empty boxes that lined one wall of her office. She joked that she probably wouldn't pack them up until the morning of her last day.

The boxes were a fitting symbol of Mulcahy's pending retirement. They spoke to an orderly, meticulously planned transition. That the boxes were still empty also reflected the fact that although Mulcahy had enjoyed nearly a decade of top leadership—far longer than the average for a CEO—the day after her retirement she would face a large void in her life where Xerox had been. To prepare herself, she had already chosen the centerpiece of her new life as serving as chair of Save the Children, which was taking her to places such as India and also to Afghanistan, a troubled spot geopolitically with high mortality rates for women and children.

As Mulcahy prepared to move on, it was clear that the legacy of her thirty-four-year career could not be put into boxes along with mementoes and photographs. Even after she has gone, her legacy would remain with the company. Fiercely competitive, with a sales rep's tenacity and determination, she had breathed new life into a company that had been all but given up for dead by analysts, advisors, and bankers. With the help of supportive directors who remained on the Xerox board after others abandoned ship, Mulcahy had found a way forward through SEC probes and the need for financing just to keep the doors open.

Even in her retirement Mulcahy was still learning and teaching others by example. Succession is not easy, and yet it is one of the most important parts of leadership and must be done well. Leaders may know intellectually that it's not about them, that they are stewards only for a time of an organization and a mission that are bigger than they are. Packing the boxes and turning off the lights are when it comes home emotionally. Then leaders can look back on the sum total of a career: what went well and what did not, the lessons learned, and how the organization benefited from their leadership.

Celebrate what you want to see more of.
　　　　　　　　　　　　　—Tom Peters,
　　　　American author and consultant

EPILOGUE:
LEARNING AND LEADING

As this book comes to a close, the lasting impression that will stay with me is the experience of having in-depth, heart-to-heart conversations with the leaders who so graciously agreed to be interviewed. When I started this project, the idea was to have a dozen or so interviews with leaders in various positions. What I didn't count on was how quickly and deeply connections would be made. I consider myself privileged to be in a position to showcase these many facets of leadership from such a diverse group of individuals.

In every conversation for this book, although leaders might refer to a note to retrieve a fact or statistic, they spoke from the heart and often from the gut. Yes, they could talk about competition, strategy, politics, sports, the arts, economics, or any other topic, but the message was never limited to what they said. The full impact came from how they made others feel. To listen to them speak was to be in the vortex of leadership at its best: the ability to move others, to get them to follow.

My own leadership has been influenced by these extraordinary individuals in dozens of ways. Similar to the leaders profiled, I am a lifelong learner. I wholeheartedly embrace the concept that learning agility—being able to learn from and adapt to changing situations—is a predictor of success. I would even go so far as to say it is a prerequisite for success. Thus having a chance to learn from a distinguished group of leaders is an accomplishment worth celebrating.

One of the lessons I learned is that leading means competing. Before my discussions with these leaders I had not consciously thought about leadership in a competitive context. Yet the hunger and desire to win—to find and inevitably punch through the opening in the sky—were present in all the leaders. They all simply loved to compete. Humbleness from victory and confidence in learning from defeat shaped them.

On closer examination, I have found the same tendencies within myself, which recall the competitive sports I played in my youth. Whether we are former athletes, are sports fans, or have challenged ourselves in other ways, such as in academics, competition calls out the best in all of us. As it is with world-class athletes, we're reminded that one rises to the level of the competition, yet true competitors mainly compete with themselves. Striving for continual improvement not only enhances personal performance, but also betters the team.

As each of the leaders demonstrated, leadership is a privilege and a responsibility, not an automatic right. No matter how lofty the office or how much prestige and access come with a title, leadership at its best should be humbling. Transparency and accessibility are absolutely necessary to motivate others.

Leaders take responsibility for what happens "on their watch" and are accountable for the results of their team. At the same time, they also delegate and empower others in order to recruit and retain talent. Motivation and inspiration are propelled by common purpose and the desire to make a difference. Self-awareness heightens a leader's ability to connect with others, to understand the emotional undercurrents in every interaction, and to motivate others to commit their passion to a common purpose.

In careers, as in life, there are significant end points and transitions. Achievements are celebrated, successes acknowledged, and failures processed for the lessons learned. Leaders are always aware that they are leading for a specific period of time, during which they are stewards of the organization. Then they will hand the baton to the next leader, who they hope will take the organization to the next level.

What also struck me in our conversations was that most of the leaders never set their sights on the top job. For them it was always about doing the best they could and focusing on the team. Eventually their innate abilities, coupled with experiences that shaped their leadership, took root with new opportunities.

From my own personal experience, becoming CEO of a NYSE-traded company was not a goal when I was younger. Yet the lessons of leadership were always around me, particularly in my youth from my dad, coaches, and teachers, and from competitive sports. I remember the wise words of my dad, who used to say that leadership has very little to do with intellect, but a lot to do with listening and learning. I can trace my commitment to lifelong learning to him; no matter how much you know (or think you know) there is still so much more that you don't. As for the listening piece, he demonstrated this wisdom in every interaction, putting more focus on others than on himself. People who do more talking than listening are closing their ears as well as their minds.

The temptation is always to have a preconceived idea of what others are thinking. Colleagues and employees, however, need to be heard first. They deserve the respect of expressing their thoughts, ideas, and challenges to a patient and attentive listener. To me it comes down to listen and learn and then lead. Without the first two actions, I cannot be effective in the third.

Leadership is never about the leader as an individual, it is about the team, the organization, the enterprise as a whole. The role of the leader is to empower and inspire others to achieve more than they could on their own—perhaps even more than they thought possible.

Empowerment needs to be more than words; it must be tangible and clearly felt. Leaders help guide others to the opportunity and then allow them to seize it. Like a good coach, the leader can correct the course, but should not micromanage. The leader needs to display confidence in the players' abilities.

Belief in one's team is the ultimate inspiration. When the leader says, "I know you can do this," people excel. They, too, will believe in the improbable. As they progress, they know the leader will always journey with them, sometimes in front, sometimes behind, but many times at their side. Change will not just be something to believe in, it will be something to experience. Encouragement will be perpetual. As progress is made, there will be recognition and celebration. People will be acknowledged genuinely in a way that touches their hearts and simultaneously reveals the leader's soul. Then together, humbly savoring success from the last peak as well as learning from the last defeat, they will carry on the journey.

NOTES

Introduction

1. Thinkexist.com, "John Wooden Quotes," http://thinkexist.com/ quotation/success_is_never_final-failure_is_never_fatal-it/148166.html.
2. Thinkexist.com, "Henry Ford Quotes," http://thinkexist.com/quotation/ failure_is_simply_the_opportunity_to_begin_again/13636.html.
3. QuotationsBook.com, "Warren Bennis Quotes," http://quotations book.com/quote/22783.

Chapter One

1. NYC.gov, "Biography," www.nyc.gov/portal/site/nycgov/menuitem .e985cf5219821bc3f7393cd401c789a0.

Chapter Seven

1. Forbes.com, "The World's Billionaires," March 10, 2010, www .forbes.com/lists/2010/10/billionaires-2010_The-Worlds-Billionaires_ Rank.html.
2. CarlosSlim.com, "The Ten Grupo Carso Principles," www.carlosslim .com/desde_ing.html#losdiez.
3. Judith H. Dobrzynski, "International Philanthropy," Carnegie Corporation of New York, 2009, http://carnegie.org/publications/ carnegie-reporter/single/view/article/item/189.

Chapter Eight

1. Ling Zhijun, *The Lenovo Affair: The Growth of China's Computer Giant and Its Takeover of IBM-PC,* trans. Martha Avery (San Francisco: Wiley, 2006), 2.
2. Ibid, 9.
3. Ibid, 11.
4. David Barboza, "An Unknown Giant Flexes Its Muscles," *The New York Times,* December 4, 2004, www.nytimes.com/2004/12/04/business/worldbusiness/04asia.html.
5. Ling, 41.

Chapter Nine

1. Forbes.com, "Daniel Vasella," http://people.forbes.com/profile/daniel-vasella/58771.

Chapter Ten

1. Geraldine Fabrikant, "Harvard and Yale Report Losses in Endowments," *The New York Times*, September 11, 2009, www.nytimes.com/2009/09/11/business/11harvard.html?_r=2&scp=4&sq=harvard%20fabrkant%202009&st=cse.
2. Drew Gilpin Faust, "Living History," *Harvard Magazine*, May 2003, http://harvardmagazine.com/2003/05/living-history.html.
3. Colleen Walsh, "Faust Bids Farewell to Class of 2008," *Harvard Gazette*, June 3, 2008, http://news.harvard.edu/gazette/story/2008/06/faust-bids-farewell-to-class-of-2008.

Chapter Eleven

1. Nokia.com, "Nokia Appoints Stephen Elop President and CEO as of September 21, 2010," September 10, 2010, www.nokia.com/press/press-releases/showpressrelease?newsid=1443731.
2. Nokia.com, "Quarterly and Annual Information, Nokia Q2 2010," July 22, 2010, www.nokia.com/about-nokia/financials/quarterly-and-annual-information/q2–2010.

ABOUT THE AUTHOR

Gary Burnison is chief executive officer of Korn/Ferry International, the world's largest executive recruiting firm and a top talent management organization. He is also a member of the firm's Board of Directors.

Burnison is a regular contributor to CNBC, CNN, and Fox Business, as well as other international news outlets. He lives in Los Angeles with his wife Leslie and children.

INDEX